Aged Care Who Cares?

Where? How? & How Much?

Rachel Lane
Noel Whittaker

16pt

Copyright Page from the Original Book

AGED CARE WHO CARES?
First published in Australia in 2011 by
Simon & Schuster (Australia) Pty Limited
Suite 19A, Level 1, 450–476 Miller St, Cammeray NSW 2062

A CBS Company
Sydney New York London Toronto

Visit our website at www.simonandschuster.com.au

© Rachel Lane and Noel Whittaker Holdings Pty Ltd 2011

All rights reserved. No part of this publication may be reproduced, stored in a retrieval system, or transmitted in any form or by any means, electronic, mechanical, photocopying, recording or otherwise, without the prior written permission of the publisher.

National Library of Australia
Cataloguing-in-Publication data:
    Lane, Rachel Kyla, 1977–
    Aged care, who cares? : Where? How? & How much? / by Rachel Lane and Noel Whittaker.

    1st ed.
    Includes index.
    9780987082954 (pbk.)

    1. Older people, Care - Australia. 2. Older people, Housing - Australia.
    3. Older people, Services for - Australia. 4. Retirement, Economic aspects - Australia.

    Other Authors/Contributors:
    Whittaker, Noel, 1940–

    362.610994

Cover design by Sharon Felschow, dta studio
Typeset in Australia by dta studio, Brendale, Queensland, 4500
Printed in Australia by McPhersons Printing Group, Victoria
Photograph of Noel Whittaker by Shane Holzberger
Cover Illustration and Cartoons by Paul Lennon

10 9 8 7 6 5 4 3 2 1

TABLE OF CONTENTS

Other titles by Noel Whittaker:	i
About the authors	iii
Acknowledgements	vi
Introduction	vii
SECTION 1: Growing old at home, plus ACAT	**1**
Chapter 1: The granny flat—rights & wrongs	2
Chapter 2: Care in your own home	14
Chapter 3: Your ACAT assessment	22
SECTION 2: Retirement villages & other options	**25**
Chapter 4: Retirement villages ... no more ladders!	28
Chapter 5: Church, charity & rental villages	37
Chapter 6: Demountable Homes Parks	43
Chapter 7: Title deeds & what lies behind	51
Chapter 8: Retirement village costs	61
Chapter 9: Retirement villages—summing up the choices	73
SECTION 3: Residential aged care	**77**
Chapter 10: Residential aged care—setting the standards	79
Chapter 11: Special services within residential aged care	89
Chapter 12: Finding the right aged care facility	99
Chapter 13: The assets assessment process	110
Chapter 14: How the government funds aged care & supported residents	121
Chapter 15: Your legal contract for aged care	128
Chapter 16: Accommodation bonds, charges & retention	137
Chapter 17: Daily care fees & income tested fees	154
SECTION 4: Financial strategies for residential aged care	**171**
Chapter 18: Keeping the former home	173
Chapter 19: Reverse Mortgages	185
Chapter 20: Using a trust or company structure	195
Chapter 21: Annuities & other income streams	206
Chapter 22: Why pay a bigger accommodation bond?	213
Chapter 23: When to go it alone	224

Chapter 24: Better to give & receive	230
Chapter 25: Meeting funeral costs	236
SECTION 5: Appendix	241
Resources	243
Directory Guide	261
Glossary	266
Do you need even more information?	281
Back Cover Material	282
Index	285

Other titles by Noel Whittaker:

MORE MONEY WITH NOEL WHITTAKER • GETTING IT TOGETHER • LIVING WELL IN RETIREMENT • GOLDEN RULES OF WEALTH • CONTROLLING YOUR CREDIT CARDS • SHARES MADE SIMPLE • SUPERANNUATION MADE SIMPLE • DRIVING SMALL BUSINESS • BORROWING TO INVEST • LOANS MADE SIMPLE • MONEY TIPS • SUPERANNUATION MADE EASY • 25 ESSENTIAL SITES FOR MASTERING YOUR MONEY • 25 ESSENTIAL SITES FOR MASTERING SMALL BUSINESS • 25 ESSENTIAL SITES FOR MASTERING YOUR LIFE • SAVING TAX ON YOUR INVESTMENT PROPERTY • BEGINNER'S GUIDE TO WEALTH

For more information visit www.agedcarewhocares.com.au

Dedicated to the senior citizens of Australia—you have earned the right to quality aged care choices.

The laws relating to superannuation, taxation, social security benefits, and the investment and handling of money, are constantly changing and are often subject to departmental discretion. While every care has been taken to ensure the accuracy of the material contained herein at the time of publication, neither the author nor the publisher will bear responsibility or liability for any action taken by any person, persons or organisation on the purported basis of information contained herein.

Without limiting the generality of the foregoing, no person, persons or organisation should invest monies or take other action on reliance of the material contained herein, but instead should satisfy themselves independently (whether by expert advice or otherwise) of the appropriateness of any such action.

About the authors

RACHEL LANE is the Executive Manager—Aged Care Solutions for Colonial First State. Having worked in financial services for 12 years and as a specialist in aged care for the past seven years, she is well known and respected within these industries, particularly for providing advice on the structuring of assets and income for aged care residents.

She regularly facilitates workshops for Aged Care Association Australia (ACAA), and is highly sought after as a presenter at aged care conferences and seminars around the country. Consulted by key industry, government and media professionals for expert comment and advice, she has had a number of articles on aged care planning published in specialist and consumer media. In addition to a full work schedule, Rachel has recently completed a Masters degree in Financial Planning.

Rachel describes herself as passionate about aged care and believes this special sphere of interest developed from the close relationship she enjoyed with her own grandmother when she was growing up.

NOEL WHITTAKER is one of Australia's best known financial advisers and is a founding director of Whittaker Macnaught Pty Ltd, a leading financial planning organisation.

Noel was made a member of the Order of Australia on Australia Day 2011 for service to the community in raising awareness of personal responsibility in matters of superannuation, household budgeting and estate planning. In 2003 he was awarded an Australian Centenary Medal for his contribution to financial services.

He is a pioneer in the field of consumer education and is the author of 19 books including the international best sellers *Making Money Made Simple* and *More Money with Noel Whittaker*. He writes weekly columns in many major Australian newspapers including the *Sydney Morning Herald*, Brisbane *Sunday Mail*, Perth *Sunday Times* and the Brisbane *Courier-Mail*. He also appears regularly on over 50 ABC radio stations and makes regular appearances on television. He is in demand as a motivational speaker and has addressed large audiences in Australia and overseas.

With over 45 years experience in the finance industry, Noel remains a director of Whittaker Macnaught and dedicates his spare time to providing financial and social commentary. He is married with three children and his hobbies are gardening and golf. His special interest is studying what makes people happy.

Acknowledgements

There is a huge amount of work involved in writing a book, especially when the subject is as complex as aged care. We are indebted to Helen Birch for the many hours spent in editing and to Linda Stewart, and Geraldine Whittaker for proof reading. The cover design and typesetting were done by Sharon Felschow who, as ever, went out of her way to make sure things proceeded smoothly and efficiently. The cartoons were drawn by Paul Lennon, one of Australia's top cartoonists and once again the printing was done by McPherson's Print Group. We are also indebted to the great people at Simon & Schuster for their input and guidance.

Introduction

In many homes the discussion topic around the family barbecue is either "what to do about the parents", or, among the older generation, "Thought about what you'll do when the house gets too much for you?"

Age is inevitable. It comes to all of us if we are lucky. What distinguishes us is, however, how we plan for it. And a key element in the plan is the appropriate aged care.

This book is intended for those who wish to secure the best possible outcome for aged care ... whether it is care for themselves or for loved ones. In it we examine some of the legal and financial implications of the various accommodation options for older people ... including the full range of options within residential aged care facilities, as well as granny flats and life tenancies, retirement villages, and caravan parks.

It can be a difficult time for older people who are facing change in their living arrangements, as well as for their adult children and other family members. There are complex rules and regulations to cope with and varying expectations of the eventual outcome. Making the wrong decisions can come at a high cost, emotionally and financially.

This is a guide on how to cut through the red tape and re-arrange the older person's financial affairs to deliver the best outcome both financially and emotionally.

The book is divided into five sections—Secton 1 covers care in the home; Section 2, retirement villages and other similar options; Section 3, aged care facilities; and Section 4, financial strategies for affordable aged care; with Section 5 giving you reference material and contacts details for further information.

We hope that this information helps you to plan your lifestyle and aged care in later years, whether you remain in your own home or choose to live in a granny flat, retirement village or an aged care facility, and that the options you choose will meet your financial needs and objectives, while giving you access to the type of care required.

The information contained in this book is current as at 1 July 2011.

SECTION I

Growing old at home, plus ACAT

For many of us the goal in old age will be to remain living independently at home or with close family members for as long as possible. The chapters in this section explore some of those options including granny flats (whether for grandad or grandma!) and the implications of granny flat rights or what is known as a life interest, and the kinds of care packages you can access that will enable you to stay longer in your own home.

This section also contains a chapter on ACAT—the assessment process carried out by an Aged Care Assessment Team to determine which government-funded aged care services you may be eligible for. We have introduced ACAT to you at this stage in the book because it applies to some of the services you can receive in your own home. However, its most important role in your life will probably come when you are considering a residential aged care facility. From time to time, we will remind you to refer back to this chapter.

Chapter 1

The granny flat—rights & wrongs

"Mum's very happy in her own little granny flat." Sounds like the perfect arrangement with Mum—or Dad or both parents—enjoying their own private space but within the property occupied by an adult child who is close at hand should they need help. But such an arrangement embodies significant legal and financial issues, including social security implications. It is very important that these are understood and addressed, if you and your loved ones are to avoid potential problems in the future.

What exactly is a granny flat? Many people think of a granny flat as a small flat built in the backyard or semi-detached to the main home but a granny flat—and with it what is known as a granny flat right or granny flat life interest—can be established within an existing home. Often such arrangements are made when parents move in with their children. This often requires the home to be modified to enable the parents to live there comfortably and safely. Common changes that need to be made include widening door frames, installing grab rails in bathrooms and showers and replacing stairs with ramps.

> A granny flat right is typically an arrangement made within a family where accommodation is provided in exchange for a payment or transfer of assets. Under social security provisions individuals are allowed to transfer assets in excess of the allowable gifting limits, to another person, in exchange for a right of occupancy in a residential property. Relatively high levels of assets can be transferred in this way, before running the risk of being caught under the avoidance provisions of the income and assets test limits.

There are generally three ways in which a granny flat right or life interest is established:
1. The parents sell their home and pay for a self-contained unit to be built on the children's property, or cover the cost of modifications to the existing home.
2. The parents remain living in their home and have the children move in to provide companionship and care, and transfer the title of the home to the children.
3. Both the parents and the children sell their existing homes and purchase a new home in the children's names.

Note: If the parents retain or have ownership of the property a granny flat *right or life interest has **NOT** been established.*

The establishment of a granny flat often comes about after the death of one parent, or clear signs of the deteriorating health of one or both parents. Payment for a granny flat right is often the purchase of a new Principal Place of Residence (PPR). However, the amount paid is known as an entry contribution—**if it is less than $135,000 you are a non-home-owner** for Centrelink purposes with the asset value assessable; if it is greater, you are a homeowner with the asset exempt.

If the former home is sold and exchanged for the granny flat right, then pension entitlement would remain unchanged as the asset position would remain the same.

If the former home is sold and a granny flat right is purchased for less than the sale proceeds, any money not used towards the granny flat right would become an assessable asset and (if kept in financial assets) would be deemed to earn income. If the assessable assets are greater than the asset threshold ($186,750 for homeowners and $321,750 for non-homeowners as at 1/7/2011) the pension entitlement will be reduced by $1.50 per $1,000 of assets in excess. If the assessable assets are financial (bank accounts, term deposits, shares etc) then even if the assets are under the asset threshold it will be important to consider the income test. The current income thresholds are $3,900p.a. for a single and

$6,864p.a. for a couple. Based on the current deeming rates, this means that for singles with financial assets over about $101,500 and for couples with more than $177,000 (and no other forms of income) the deemed income will exceed the threshold, causing a reduction in pension entitlement at 50¢ per dollar.

If the proceeds from the sale of the home and assets outside the home are used to purchase the granny flat, the pension entitlement would likely increase. However there are limits around this and once the limits are exceeded the amount above the limit will be treated as a gift.

How much is too much?

Generally speaking the amount you pay for a granny flat right or life interest is considered to be the market price. This is because they are family arrangements and it can be difficult to place a value on them. However, in some circumstances a reasonableness test can be applied to a granny flat right or life interest. Any amount paid in excess of the test can be considered a deprived asset. Centrelink uses this term for gifting in excess of the allowed amounts, i.e. when someone transfer assets for less than their market value or, as in this case when parents pay an excessive amount for their granny flat rights, when they do not receive adequate consideration for the gift they are making.

The reasonableness test will be applied where:
- Someone transfers the title to their home (or purchases property in another person's name) and transfers additional assets
- Someone pays for the cost of construction and transfers additional assets
- It is considered that the person is establishing a granny flat right to gain a social security advantage.

The reasonableness test amount is calculated by multiplying the combined annual couple rate of pension (on the date the right was established) by the relevant conversion factor (refer to table on pages 6 and 7). This formula is used irrespective of the person's couple status, i.e. the same amount is used for a single person as it is for a couple. When calculating the amount for a couple, the age next birthday of the youngest member is used.

Where someone has transferred the title and additional assets or covered the cost of construction and transferred additional assets, the amount paid is compared to the reasonableness amount and the higher of the two is taken to be the value of the granny flat right, with the excess being a gift. However, where it is considered that the person is establishing a granny flat right to obtain a social security advantage, the granny flat right is equal to the reasonableness test.

Watch out for this one: if someone needs to vacate a granny flat within five years of it being established and the reason that they need to leave would have been anticipated at the time the granny flat right was established, the value of the granny flat right will be considered a deprived asset.

Case Study

Jenny is 77 and recently widowed. She needs some assistance with her daily activities and cannot drive (things her husband used to assist her with).

Her Assets are:
- House $450,000
- Cash $60,000
- Contents $2,000

If Jenny covers the cost of constructing a granny flat ($150,000) in her children's home and also gives her children $300,000 her granny flat right will be compared to the reasonableness amount of $316,143. This is calculated as 11.06 (valuation factor for age next birthday of 78) x couple pension. Her cost of construction will be compared to the reasonableness amount and the greater of the two will be considered to be her granny flat interest. In this case her granny flat right will have a value of $316,143 and the remaining monies $133,857 will be considered a gift. Due to the deemed income from the gift and her bank accounts, her pension will be reduced by around $80.00 per fortnight.

What happens later on?

While the idea of the family looking after their ageing members is certainly not a new concept, the complexities of such arrangements are often overlooked. Children and parents may start off with the best of intentions but are often working on the basis of unspoken expectations. Too often they realise the differences in these expectations when confronted with a new situation months or years down the track. The situation is normally one that could have reasonably been foreseen, but the expectations of what would happen in that situation are completely different.

What will happen if the children wish to go on holidays? What will happen if the parent's care needs change and they cannot be safely looked after in the home? Who should pay for the cost of care? Will the parent make a contribution to household expenses such as food, utilities and insurance? Of course if the living arrangement continues for many years it may be necessary to consider what the consequences would be if the adult children divorce, or if one of those caring for the parent became ill or passed away.

Because in many cases the purchase of the granny flat right is coming from the sale of the family home (or the transfer of the home) disputes often erupt amongst siblings who, although happy to concede that they are unable or unwilling to look after their ageing parents, have a vested interest in the family home as the largest asset in the future estate.

If the person's age next birthday is	Then use this Conversion Factor
51	33.30
52	32.39
53	31.47
54	30.56
55	29.65
56	28.74
57	27.85
58	26.95
59	26.07
60	25.19
61	24.32
62	23.45
63	22.60
64	21.75
65	20.91
66	20.08
67	19.26
68	18.46

69	17.66
70	16.87
71	16.09
72	15.33
73	14.58
74	13.84
75	13.12
76	12.41
77	11.73
78	11.06
79	10.42
80	9.80
81	9.20
82	8.62
83	8.06
84	7.53
85	7.03
86	6.56
87	6.11
88	5.69
89	5.31
90	4.96
91	4.64
92	4.34
93	4.08
94	3.84
95	3.63

96	3.45
97	3.28
98	3.13
99	3.00
100+	2.88

To try to please everyone a parent may decide to transfer only part of the value of the home and amend their will so that the part they retain is given to the other children when they pass away. As a result they become tenants in common with the children who are looking after them. In these circumstances what they have established is not considered to be a granny flat right because they still have legal ownership of part of the property. This can have implications for their pension and the cost of residential aged care if this is required in the future.

For all these reasons it is important to seek legal and financial advice to understand the implications of the agreement you are entering into, whether as a parent or child, and to provide certainty and transparency of the details. Although Centrelink does not require a legal document to accept that a granny flat right has been established, they do recommend that people consult their solicitor and perhaps have a document prepared to give evidence of a life tenancy or interest. It might seem strange to have a legal document to protect your rights in a family matter but it could save problems and unpleasant arguments in the future.

Informal care—the kind of care provided by family members to older relatives which might include assistance with communication, paperwork, mobility, cognitive tasks, emotional support and transport—was provided by an estimated 2.3 million people in 2006. Access Economics have estimated that the replacement of informal care with formal care would have cost an estimated $40 billion per annum in 2010!

> *While often the intention with these granny flat arrangements is for the family to provide care and support to their ageing loved one, it may be necessary at some point to access care in the home or respite services. Community Aged Care Packages (CACPs) or Home And Community Care Packages (HACC) may be able to be accessed to assist with personal care, meals,*

cleaning etc. We'll look at these in the next chapter.

Chapter 2

Care in your own home

Many of us think of aged care as a service provided in an aged care facility but in fact most people access aged care in their own home. In 2009–10 around 69,000 people received a Community Aged Care Package (CACP) and around 616,000 people aged over 70 received services via Home and Community Care packages (HACC).

CACPs and HACC packages are designed to assist people who would prefer to continue living in their own home and community. The packages can be delivered in their own home, caravan park, retirement village, granny flat and many other forms of living arrangement.

There are three types of community care packages subsidised by the Australian Government:
- Community Aged Care Packages (CACPs)
- Extended Aged Care at Home (EACH) and
- Extended Aged Care at Home Dementia (EACHD).

CACPs, EACH & EACHD

Let's assume that you are in need of some care to remain living in your present home. The care package that you receive will be tailored to your specific needs by your care manager. It is their role to plan and manage your package from a range of services covering assistance with personal care such as showering and dressing; domestic assistance such as preparation of meals; assistance with laundry, shopping, housework and gardening; and transport to social activities or doctors' appointments. CACPs generally provide around 5–6 hours per week of assistance.

To be eligible to receive one of these packages you will need to have an assessment by an Aged Care Assessment Team (usually just referred to as an ACAT). A description of this process is given in the next chapter.

You will be expected to pay a contribution towards the cost of your care package if you can afford it. You should agree on the fee associated with your CACP with your service provider before you start receiving the service.

If you are a pensioner you cannot be charged more than 17.5% of that pension. If you have a higher income you may be asked to pay more, but it cannot exceed 50% of the higher income or the capped maximum. If you cannot afford to pay, however, you will not be denied a service.

The maximum fee for CACPs changes each 20 March and 20 September. For pensioners this fee, as at 20 March 2011, is $8.38 per day.

The subsidies that the service providers receive are set on 1 July each year and are paid directly to them through Medicare. As at 1 July 2011 the daily CACP subsidy was $36.73. The subsidy paid for EACH was $122.79 per day and for EACHD $135.41.

HACC packages

HACC packages, like CACPs, are designed to provide assistance to older people to continue living in their own home and community. At present HACC services are funded by the Australian and state and territory governments on a lump sum basis to the provider. The provider of the services then undertakes the assessment of those requiring services on a needs basis. HACC services generally provide less support than CACPs, with most people receiving around two hours of support per week.

HACC fees and charges are based on the service provided and the level of income of the person receiving the package. The following table is an example of the fees and charges for HACC services in metro Victoria.

HACC fees effective 1 January 2011 (Metropolian Victoria)

Service type	Low fee (max. to be charged)	Medium fee (max. to be charged)	High fee (max. to be charged) Full cost recovery
Planned Activity Group includes PAG core and PAG high	$6.80 per day (plus cost of meal if bought from another source)	As for low fee	$11.90 (core) $16.80 (high) (per hour plus cost of meal if bought from another source)
Allied Health Services (Dietetics, Occupational Therapy, Podiatry, Physiotherapy, Speech Therapy, Counselling)	$8.80 per consultation	$13.50 per consultation	$89.10 per hour*
Domestic assistance*	$5.40 per hour	$13.50 per hour	$29.30 per hour
Property maintenance*	$10.80 per hour (plus cost of materials)	$16.20 per hour (plus cost of materials)	$42.70 per hour (plus cost of materials)
Personal care*	$4.10 per hour	$8.10 per hour	$33.50 per hour
Respite*	$2.70 per hour	$4.10 per hour	$30.30 per hour
Nursing (includes district nursing)	$3.40 per visit	$29.70 per hour*	$81.60 per hour*

| Linkages | Fee will be based on the relevant HACC activity provided as part of the package. Also refer to the HACC program manual. | As for low fee range | As for low fee range |

*Fee should be applied pro rata when part hour services are provided.

Client contribution to cost of activity

| Delivered meals | $8.10 per meal | As per low range | Full cost of recovery |
| Bush nursing | Subscription | Subscription | Subscription |

HACC income ranges 2011

	Low	Medium		High
Individual	< $34,232	> $34,232	< $73,334	> $73,334
Couple	< $55,692	> $55,692	< $98,036	> $98,036
Family (1 child)	< $61,225	> $61,225	< $103,240	> $103,240
	(plus $5,533 per additional child)			

Veterans' Home Care (VHC) and Community Nursing Programs

In 2009–10 69,600 veterans over 70 accessed a VHC package and 31,400 received community nursing. In addition to other in-home care packages, the Australian Government through the Department of Veterans' Affairs (DVA) offers a range of services for veterans and war widows/widowers.

Veterans' Home Care packages can include personal care, domestic assistance, safety related home and garden maintenance and respite care. If you are eligible for VHC, you can choose whether to receive your services through VHC or HACC or through both programs (as long as there is no doubling up of the services provided). Services received through HACC and/or VHC are charged at the rate applicable to the particular service provider; VHC clients may find they are better off with VHC rates.

To be eligible to receive VHC services you must be a veteran of the Australian defence forces or a war widow(er) of a veteran and have a Gold or White Repatriation Health Card. A small co-payment is normally required and there may be a limit on the amount of the service you can access.

The following are the current co-payment arrangements (as at 1 July 2011):
- **Personal Care**—$5 per hour, maximum $10 per week
- **Domestic Assistance**—$5 per hour, maximum $5 per week
- **Home and Garden Maintenance**—$5 per hour, each hour of service
- **Respite Services**—no co-payment applies

People who cannot afford to meet the cost of the co-payment can apply under financial hardship to DVA to waive their fees.

The assessment for VHC packages is conducted by the regional VHC assessment agency. You can be referred to this service by your doctor or other medical professional or you can arrange the assessment yourself by calling 1300 550 450.

Private Carers

The ageing population has seen a huge increase in demand for in-home care services. Often private care services are used as a "top up" to government subsidised services provided through CACPs and HACC packages.

The services you can access through these private carers will vary from one service provider to another, and so will the cost. Generally speaking, the services that are provided on a domestic assistance basis (assistance with meals, participation in activities such as crafts, collecting prescriptions/dry cleaning and housekeeping) are less expensive than services that require medical supervision (such as assistance with changing dressings, administering medications etc).

In some circumstances these services will come from the same provider involved in a CACP or HACC package. If this is the case it is best to discuss the total package with them and let them build a care plan around your needs and the services for which you can get funding.

Chapter 3
Your ACAT assessment

The term "ACAT" (Aged Care Assessment Team) is one you will come across repeatedly as you learn more about aged care services. The ACAT Assessment is the key to accessing many of the Government funded aged care services, including CACPs, EACH, Respite and permanent Residential Aged Care. ACAT Assessments are free and can be carried out in your home or at the ACAT offices (normally within a hospital).

The idea of being assessed by a stranger or a group of strangers can be very daunting. Knowing your rights and what will happen when and why can help alleviate some of this anxiety. It is also a good idea to have a family member, carer or friend present and, if you wish, you can have an independent advocate attend the meeting with you. If you need an interpreter you can bring one, or the ACAT can arrange to have one in attendance.

The ACAT is a team of people that includes doctors, nurses, social workers and therapists. In most cases you will have contact with one or two people only who will speak to you about your day-to-day activities, the things you are comfortable doing for yourself and the things you may need assistance with. These questions could range from how easily you are coping with showering or bathing to difficulties you might be having in carrying the shopping home. They will also ask you questions about your general health and may request a copy of your medical history from your doctor. During this meeting you will be given the opportunity to express your ideas about your care needs.

This information will be used to determine what your care needs are and which care service(s) will be best for you. You will receive written confirmation of the outcome of your assessment including reasons why the ACAT have made their decisions and the services for which you have been approved. They will also provide you with information about service providers in your area.

It's important to keep your complete copy of the ACAT assessment, known as the Aged Care Client Record (ACCR), as you need to show this document to aged care service providers to confirm that you are eligible for their services.

If you are unhappy with your assessment you should discuss any concerns with the person in charge of the ACAT Team. If the assessment determines that you are not eligible to receive aged care services, or you need to escalate your issue, you can lodge an appeal.

Your ACAT Assessment will remain valid indefinitely if you receive a high-level care service—EACH, EACHD or permanent residential care.

You will need to be re-assessed by the ACAT within 12 months if you have been approved for but not received low level care services—CACP or permanent residential care.

If you have been approved for a transition care program but not received it you will need to be re-assessed within four weeks.

If you are receiving care in your home you will only need to be reassessed if your care needs change.

If you are living in an aged care facility, they will manage your assessments unless your care needs change—most commonly, from low care to high care—and you need to move from your one facility to another to receive the appropriate care. In this instance a new ACAT assessment may be necessary.

> *Most people are referred to ACAT by their doctor, community nurse or social worker but you—or a family member—are free to make direct contact with ACAT yourself. Rest assured that the ACAT interview process is a relatively easy one and the team's objective is to help you. Bear in mind, however, that in some cases you could be waiting up to six weeks or more to get an appointment for the assessment to be carried out.*

SECTION 2

Retirement villages & other options

These days it can be difficult to distinguish between a retirement village, caravan park and demountable homes park. In fact in some cases it can be difficult to distinguish between some of these arrangements and an aged care facility. Many terms are used across a range of different developments, each with their own financial and legal structures. Such terms include "Lifestyle Village", "Supported Living Community", "Assisted Living Neighbourhood" and "Retirement Resort".

However, as you will see, the distinctions are important in considering which arrangement is the right one for you.

Retirement villages operate under the relevant state or territory legislation which typically sets a minimum age of 55. This legislation generally provides a definition of what is and isn't considered to be a retirement village, sets out what legal documents (including disclosures) are required to be provided to residents by the village operator, regulates some (not all) financial arrangements and provides framework for the resolution of disputes.

Demountable Homes Parks (DHPs) or Manufactured Homes Parks are often referred as "residential parks". Like retirement villages they operate under state or territory legislation either via specific Acts such as the Manufactured Homes (Residential Parks) Act or as part of Residential Tenancies Acts or a combination of the two. While DHPs are often marketed to retirees and may appear to be age-restrictive (i.e. only for people over the age of 55), anti-discrimination laws prevent such restrictions being allowed.

Caravan Parks are often thought of as a place to visit on your way around Australia in your retirement years—the so-called Grey Nomad trail. However, in recent years many people, particularly retirees, have made a caravan park their home. The residency contract for a caravan park is likely to fall under the same legislation as a DHP and, in fact, many DHPs were born out of caravan parks, the main difference being that caravan park residents will have a rental agreement, while DHPs are much more likely to be leasehold arrangements.

All of these options are explored in this Section.

Chapter 4
Retirement villages ... no more ladders!

What springs to mind when you hear the words "retirement village"? Does it conjure up a picture of very old people sitting around waiting for the inevitable? Or do you see it as a vibrant community of active people who are so busy they hardly have time to take part in all the activities?

Rachel admits to once having a negative image of retirement villages, but then, as part of her job, she started to visit clients who were living in them. Almost without exception they were far happier and healthier than they had been in their previous home and most were sorry they had not made the change years earlier. However, the majority confessed that they had at first experienced apprehension at the thought of moving.

In reality, moving to a retirement village usually turns out to be an exciting and fulfilling experience so the aim of these chapters is to provide sufficient information for you to explore this prospect and decide if moving to a retirement village is appropriate for you.

There is no doubt that the home environment is a major influence on the happiness of older people since their lifestyle centres so much more on activities in the home.

Retirement villages generally offer two types of accommodation:
1. independent living units
2. serviced apartments/supported living units

There may be an aged care facility located on the same site as the retirement village, however the care and financial arrangements that apply are different and are covered in Section 3.

Understand first that a retirement village tends to be an option for people in their 70s and it is a choice that may arise suddenly. Certainly there is a traditional belief that people enter a retirement village because of the facilities offered, or the need to live with people of a similar kind, but in reality this is not so.

In Australia you are likely to start thinking about retirement village living when you become tired of looking after your own home, or if you have a health scare. Suddenly you become increasingly aware of your own mortality and start to mull over how you would cope if your partner died or you became disabled. The idea of moving to a retirement village then comes to the fore, because the choice is usually between that or staying in your own home.

Staying in your own home is certainly fine while you are well. But if your spouse dies there can be loneliness to cope with, and if you become disabled it may be necessary to bring in outside help to assist with cooking, cleaning and some personal care. As the years pass, the difficulties may increase and isolation from the family and community is all too common.

The tragedy is that people alone in the old family home might be clinging to what they see as "independence" but in reality are becoming increasingly dependent on the help and goodwill of others. If they moved to a retirement village they have security and freedom of choice. Their meals and laundry are provided and they can take part in activities of their choosing, yet be alone when the mood takes them. That to us is true independence—being master of your own destiny and once again being part of a community.

Therefore, it makes good sense to consider a move to a retirement village before the choice is forced on you. In a retirement village you often enjoy 24-hour emergency call care, facilities such as a bowling green, a recreational hall and a swimming pool and, best of all, you are likely to live in a close-knit community of like-minded active people who can give you support when you face the inevitable crises of life.

If you are retired, these are the factors that may swing your thoughts towards a move to a retirement village:

1. **Maintaining a house.** You may be getting tired of mowing, painting, gardening and attending to items such as rates and insurance. No more ladders for you—let someone else do the work!
2. **Social life.** Your children may be scattered throughout the country and you are starting to feel that little bit lonely. You find yourself spending more and more time in front of the television set and realise you are in danger of vegetating.
3. **Sport.** Deep down you may yearn for a game of bowls or a game of cards but don't feel confident enough to take the steps to do it.
4. **Health.** Maybe you or a friend have had a health scare and you realise it would be comforting for you to have trained help close by.

If you can recognise yourself in one or more of the above situations, you should start to explore the possibility of retirement village living. You may be confused by the range of choices but by the end of the five chapters in this Section you will understand them much better. We'll start off by discussing totally independent living in a retirement village and then move on to compare it with living in a serviced apartment or a supported living community.

Independent living

Independent living in a standard retirement village provides the lowest level of care and differs little from living in your own home. Usually you live in one- or two-bedroom cottages, or in duplex types of accommodation, and the only care offered is emergency care. Most retirement villages have a string of emergency buttons that can be used to summon help quickly.

Activities are usually centred around a recreation hall where residents meet for social pastimes such as lectures and games and, depending on the type of retirement village, there may be other facilities such as a billiard room, library, swimming pool, bowling green and tennis court. The average age of residents in Australian retirement villages is 74.

The major benefits of living here instead of in your own home are freedom from maintenance chores; no heavy expenditure such as painting your house or replacing the guttering; and the existence of emergency assistance facilities.

A big plus is the companionship of like-minded people. This is particularly important if your partner dies because, even though you have lost a major figure in your life, you have not lost the other friends around you. Thus you still have a major emotional support base at a time in your life when you need it most, and your independence and contact with your friends is not suddenly taken from you. Research shows that the network of friends a person has is a major indicator of how long and how happily they will live.

Serviced apartments/supported living units

In some retirement villages you will find at least two levels of care: independent units and serviced apartments or supported living units. A serviced apartment or supported living unit provides a higher level of assistance and here the typical resident is a woman in her early 80s. Increasing demand for care services from existing residents of retirement villages has forced many village operators into providing these services.

The level of care that can be provided to you in a retirement village will vary from one to another. Traditional retirement villages focus on lifestyle and activities and want to attract residents who are sociable and physically active. These villages may require that you leave if your health deteriorates, as too many people sitting around in wheelchairs or hibernating in their units can have a detrimental effect on the experience of the other residents, as well as the ability to sell units to new residents.

In some circumstances the village operator will allow you to have care provided to you in your unit. If the retirement village cannot organise this for you, you will need to make your own arrangements just as you would in your own home, through government funded community aged care packages or private services or a combination of the two. The ability to access care is becoming a key consideration as many people move into a village in their mid 70s, with around 60% entering as a couple. A retirement village that can provide care services or has an aged care facility located on-site is often a good solution where one member of a couple requires care but the other doesn't. These arrangements can enable them to be close together which would not be possible if the retirement village offered independent living only.

At the other end of the scale there are retirement villages that are purpose built to deliver aged care. It can be difficult to tell the difference between these and an aged care facility as the rooms are all single rooms with an ensuite and they are often built to the same specifications with wide doorways to fit wheelchairs and lifting apparatus, bathrooms with handrails and showers without a recess to enable staff to assist with showering, as well as the provision of meals, domestic services and some nursing services. These services may be delivered to you as your care needs increase or it may be a condition of entry that you already require some or all of these to be provided.

Where it is a condition of entry that you require care, the retirement village operator will generally assess your needs prior to you moving in to ensure that they can provide the appropriate services. They will generally co-ordinate the package of services for you and provide you with a price table to help you understand what the cost will be now and what you can expect if your care needs increase. In many cases the care being provided will be through a government funded community care package with the retirement village delivering any "top up" services themselves or through private contractors.

The key considerations if you are thinking about moving to one of these villages are:

1. What are my care needs now? What are they likely to be over the next 10 years? At what point can the village no longer provide the care or services I require?

2. How do I feel about living with other people that have care needs that are likely to increase?
3. How will I fund the next move?

In the next two chapters we will look at some of your other options: church and charity-run villages, rental villages, and caravan or demountable homes parks.

Chapter 5

Church, charity & rental villages

Most church and charity-based retirement villages are now little different from those run by private enterprise. They developed through government subsidies in the years after the Second World War on the understanding that they would look after the poorer members of their particular interest group. These subsidies have been phased out and the churches and charities now rely on entry contributions from residents, donations and other sources of funds to continue providing these services.

Initially, retirees preferred church-run or charity-run villages to private enterprise villages because there was a commonality of interest, but now many have long waiting lists and often they do not offer the same standards of accommodation as the modern villages run by the private operators.

Don't imagine that villages run by the churches and charities will always offer a lower entry fee. Many do but sometimes their exit fee is higher than that charged by private enterprise. Make sure you check it out. Some of the church and charity groups will let you in with an interest-free loan of as little as $40,000, but then you lose it all when you leave. For those with limited means unable to afford a market price unit, this may be the best option. But for those who can afford to choose, the **total** cost of each should be compared, rather than just focusing on the reduced entry price.

Rental villages

While traditionally the church and charitable sector has been the main provider of rental retirement accommodation, there are a few private sector rental villages around.

Rental villages tend to operate under one of two models: a subsidised rental model for people with few assets whose income is fixed and often includes entitlement to government rent assistance; and a market price model for people who choose to rent their unit, paying a higher ongoing cost but with little or no DMF (Deferred Management Fee).

The most well-known of the subsidised rental models is probably Village Life which built retirement villages for people with little or no financial means. The villages were very simple, mainly one bedroom or bedsit type units with a small kitchenette (microwave and fridge but no oven) and communal laundry facilities. The villages had a communal dining room and social areas (library or hall). The weekly fee was calculated at 85% of the full pension plus 100% of government rent assistance (approx $358p.w.) and included three meals a day and a linen/laundry service (weekly). Responsibility for personal outgoings—electricity, water, insurance and telephone—was the responsibility of the resident (presumably from the $53p.w. of pension that remained plus interest from bank accounts etc.).

A series of mergers and acquisitions saw a number of these villages placed into listed property trusts with the expectation that the ageing population would see demand for such services increase dramatically over the coming years and large profits could be made. At its peak one of the property trusts had a unit price of $2.88, from a float price of $.80. With rental income set at 85% of the pension and 100% of the Rent assistance paid by the Federal Government the villages provided an acceptable yield until real estate prices and construction costs around Australia rose dramatically in 2003–2004.

Subsequently a series of profit downgrades saw the price fall to just $0.09. A number of the villages were sold off and according to some reports more than 400 residents faced eviction from the new owners who wanted to change the financial structure to be 99 year lease with a $200,000 entry contribution.

If you are looking for a retirement village unit to rent, you should be aware that villages that consist solely of rentals tend to be very small. However, some of the larger villages will sometimes keep a number of units available on a rental basis. Because you are effectively paying the re-current charges plus rent for your unit, as well as compensating the operator for not receiving any capital upfront or DMF at the end, these arrangements can be more expensive than renting a unit outside the village. You also need to keep in mind that, just like a normal rental, you are responsible for all your personal outgoings such as food, water, electricity, insurance and telephone. And while the village may be able to provide you with meals or personal services, generally these are at an additional cost.

While rental villages often look just like a retirement village with the communal areas and social activities, you need to make sure you understand whether you are a tenant or a resident. As a tenant you will sign a Residential Tenancy Agreement, either on a fixed or periodic basis, and will be covered by the Residential Tenancies Authority. This agreement may also require you to lodge a security deposit with the Residential Tenancies Bond Authority, normally equal to four weeks rent. This legislation is the same as if you rented a private home and can be ended at any time depending on what the terms are specified in the agreement.

In a large village run by the not for profit sector, where most units are under loan licence arrangements, there can sometimes be a few set aside specifically for rent by people who are financially disadvantaged and could not afford the standard arrangement. Often these arrangements work on a combination of an upfront payment, either as an entry contribution or a donation to the church or charity, and an ongoing rent. The entry fee is normally based on the resident's ability to pay, ensuring they are left with a minimum amount of assets. The rent is normally a percentage of the full pension plus the maximum rental assistance, regardless of the actual amount the resident is entitled to receive.

In contrast to all of the licence, loan and lease arrangements a rental model may seem easier and cheaper in the long run. But the long run is the key with a rental village. As we have pointed out, some of these villages have proven to be unviable from an investor's perspective and left residents looking for other places to live or with new management that inevitably has to cut costs and services to try and turn the losses into profits.

Chapter 6

Demountable Homes Parks

In Chapter 4 we challenged your assumptions about retirement villages. Now let's turn your attention to Demountable Homes Parks. What comes to mind when you hear these words? Do you get visions of rundown, one bedroom cabins tucked away out the back of a caravan park close to the ocean with a handful of people living there and little or no community facilities besides the communal toilet and shower block? You could be in for a surprise.

DHPs can generally be classified into two groups: those that originated from caravan parks for tourist accommodation and also offer permanent sites (often in a distinct area) and those that are purpose built villages/communities normally marketed to retirees.

DHPs that originated from tourist parks often change the mix of residents depending on demand, council approval and market price. Many of these parks are in wonderful seaside locations and transforming the park from a caravan park for tourists and seasonal workers to a demountable homes park with a mix of tourists and permanent residents can mean that the operator is able to receive a higher income with greater regularity. (Until the mid 1980s in NSW it was illegal to live in a caravan park, with legislation preventing people from residing in such a park for more than 3 or 6 months in any 12-month period. This was largely due to the fact that caravans didn't meet minimum housing standards and there were concerns around health and safety. Over the years the legislation changed in each state.)

Many retirees who live in these parks enjoy a strong sense of community amongst the permanent residents, while having the ability to enjoy socialising with the passing parade of tourists. Of course the facilities built to cater to the tourists—barbecues, playgrounds, swimming pools and so on—are also popular with the residents and their visitors (particularly the grandkids).

Unfortunately, the increasing land prices along the coast have meant that many of these parks have been sold off and turned into upmarket apartments or beach houses and many retirees have been displaced.

DHPs that are purpose built for the retiree market have all the look and feel of a bricks and mortar retirement village with communal facilities such as swimming pools, bowling greens, tennis courts etc. A DHP we visited recently on Queensland's Gold Coast even had its own private cinema and a lake stocked with fish so the residents could go fishing (with a better chance of catching some dinner!)

These kinds of DHPs normally have bigger units, with the majority being two-bed units and a large proportion being three-bed units. There tend to be very few (if any) single room units and as a result there will be larger numbers of people in the village.

The units themselves can be hard to pick as demountable or relocatable homes, particularly when there is a garden surrounding them, and they come with all the mod cons: air conditioning, full kitchen, often an ensuite as well as a central bathroom, a laundry, a front deck and in some cases a back deck also. In fact, independent analysis in 2009 of the sale of homes within one DHP on Queensland's Sunshine Coast showed that the annual capital gain was 74% greater than surrounding residential housing.

DHPs are however, often cheaper than the bricks and mortar retirement village unit, largely due to the cheaper construction costs, with the cost of a new home ranging from around $150,000 to $650,000 depending on size and quality.

The key difference between a DHP and a retirement village is that the loan, licence or lease arrangement between the resident and the operator is over the land, not the building. Being an owner-occupier and a tenant at the same time poses a unique set of circumstances for people living in a DHP. Traditionally, DHPs have had no stamp duty, entry fees or exit fees and many residents of DHPs have qualified for government rent assistance. However, in those we looked at in researching this book we found that some of the new villages do charge a Deferred Management Fee (DMF) on the sale of the home.

Just like in the retirement village model, there is also a rental model within DHPs. Under these arrangements you need to pay rent for the home and rent for the land on which it sits. While the park manager will receive the rent for the land, it is possible that a separate owner receives rent for the home, effectively making you a tenant of two different people. Under these circumstances you will need enter two different residency contracts and a bond may be payable for each.

The residency agreement will cover all of the terms and conditions including the amount of rent payable, frequency of payment, the amount of security bond, the length of the tenancy, as well as details of how and when utilities are payable, along with any other rules relating to the park. As the bond is generally lodged with a government agency, such as the Residential Bond Authority, a condition report should be completed when you take possession of the property and again when you leave. Any damage (other than fair wear and tear) to the unit or communal facilities within the park or unpaid rent can be deducted from the bond.

Commonwealth Rent Assistance and DHPs

Because of the nature of ownership within a Demountable Homes Park, i.e. you own the home but rent the land (often called "site fees"), Rent Assistance is often payable to residents of these parks.

Here's how you calculate the rent assistance payable:

The rent you pay must be above the minimum threshold for rent assistance to be payable. The minimum thresholds are: $103.60 pfn for singles and $168.60 pfn for couples (different thresholds apply to couples separated due to illness or share arrangements). Rent Assistance is paid at 75% of the rent above this threshold, up to the maximum of $116.40 pfn for singles and $109.80 pfn for couples.

Case Study

Shirley is a full age pensioner living in a DHP that charges $120p.w. for site fees.

Her rent assistance will be calculated as:

Rent paid	$240.00	pfn
Minus threshold	$103.60	pfn
Excess	$136.40	pfn
× 75% =	$102.30	pfn

Rent Assistance paid would be $102.30 *pfn*

If Shirley's site fees were $150p.w., her rent assistance would calculate as $147.30 pfn but the maximum rent assistance payable is $116.40 pfn so that is the amount she would be paid.

The fact that rent assistance is payable under these arrangements has caused accusations of artificial inflation of the site fees as park owners expect that the majority of residents will be able to claim the rent assistance and therefore can afford a higher amount of site fees or the owners set the site fees at the amount at which maximum rent assistance is payable.

Increasing rents

One of the main concerns for resident of Demountable Homes Parks and Caravan Parks is increases to the site fees (rent) that they need to pay. Often the leases offered within the park vary from one resident to another, and while the lease will indicate the rate at which the rent will be increased during the period of the lease (e.g. CPI) for those with shorter leases the expiry of the lease can bring great uncertainty about the affordability of the new lease.

Notice to leave

In certain circumstances the park owner or manager has the power to serve the resident with a notice to leave the premises. A notice to leave means that the person given the notice must leave the premises and cannot return for a given period of time (normally between one and three days). The reasons for giving such a notice include deliberately causing damage to the caravan or park, serious disruptions of the peace and enjoyment of the park for other residents or visitors or any act that could put other residents or visitors or the park in danger.

Notice to vacate

A notice to vacate is an order to leave permanently and can be issued, normally by providing at minimum a week's notice, for failing to pay rent, using the site for illegal purposes or continual breaches as above. Where the home or caravan is to be or has been sold, 60 days' notice must be provided. If the park as a whole is being sold, closing down or is being re-developed, 6 months' notice is needed. Residents have the right to challenge any of these orders through the relevant states' tribunal process.

Chapter 7
Title deeds & what lies behind

Now you understand about different levels of care we can move on to the technical stuff. In this chapter we look at the various forms of titles that exist for retirement villages and what these mean in terms of your rights.

In general terms, there are four different types of retirement village title but you may find that some villages have a mixture of leasehold and licensed arrangements in a single scheme:

1. leasehold
2. licence
3. company title
4. freehold title.

Each of the above gives you secure occupancy of your unit but we believe the most important considerations are the philosophy, resources and skill of the developer.

In the past most developers offered only one level of care, i.e. independent living in a retirement village. However, the age at which people move into villages has been older than many developers expected and a growing number of residents have needed to access care during their stay in the village, either for themselves or their partner. Villages built with a longer-term view and a philosophy that they should offer a wide choice of care levels began to provide residential aged care on site.

Remember the supported living units we mentioned in Chapter 4 and the convenience of having an aged care facility in proximity to the retirement village? Residents of independent living units today often want aged care support in their unit, with the ability to move to the aged care facility if that becomes necessary.

It makes sense to stay in the one village if at all possible to maintain your friendship network. However, one of the lessons that both developers and residents of retirement villages have learned in recent years is that, while this may seem like a great solution, financially it may mean that it is much harder to gain access to the aged care facility when you need to. Over the past eight years accommodation bonds in aged care facilities have gone from a government set amount of around $120,000 to be more in line with a market price model, with average bonds in most capital cities around $300,000 or more. During this time residents of retirement villages have also seen the value of their units increase of course but at nowhere near the same rate—once the Deferred Management Fee (DMF) is taken from the sale price, some residents find themselves priced out of the accommodation bond market.

Some retirement villages operate purely on a strata title basis and are only interested in selling units. As a result, there may be no on-site care or ongoing management. If you buy into a retirement village that runs on this philosophy, you may find life little different from living in a large strata titled apartment block such as you may find almost anywhere in Australia. This type of strata title retirement village was once popular in Sydney but is becoming less attractive as people realise the problems that can develop as the residents get older and become less capable of looking after themselves and the affairs of their village.

What is important is that you seek a developer/operator who has the skills to build a first-class retirement complex, and the resources and skill to run it over the long haul—in other words, one who will stay around to deliver what is promised.

Now let's look at these title deeds in more detail.

Leasehold

This is probably the most common form of title. When you move into the village you pay an agreed sum in exchange for a 99-year lease on the unit. This lease naturally lasts for your lifetime and, if a couple take out the lease and one dies, it continues to the death of the other partner. Your lease is registered on the title deed but when you die the rights die with you. You cannot pass the rights under that lease onto your children even if they are approaching retirement age themselves.

Licence

In some villages the right to occupy the unit is granted by a licence instead of a lease. You lend the developer an agreed sum and in return you are allowed to live in the property. You are still entitled to live in the unit for life but, unlike a lease, the licence is not registered on the title deed. However, your rights under the licence are recognised by law, so effectively you are in the same position as if you had a registered lease.

Company title

Under company title you buy shares in a company that has an interest in the village and your share gives you the right to occupy a certain unit and to use the common property of the village.

Freehold title

If you buy freehold title you become the owner of the property, in strata title or group title, and have the title deed registered in your name. Be aware this is not quite the same as owning your own home because the developer may restrict the right to sell it to someone who does not meet the developer's guidelines. Furthermore, you may be liable for a DMF when you leave. This topic is covered in detail later. However, your family have the right to occupy it when you die if they meet the developer's guidelines.

If you think about the above four options you will find they fall into two main categories:

1. **Lease, licence or company title** which gives you secure rights of occupancy but leaves ownership with the operator/developer of the village. You still pay a sum up-front and you may, or may not, get most if it back when you leave.

    Leasehold and licence arrangements are common because they enable developers to retain control over the village and spare residents the worry of trying to sell their units when they leave. Furthermore, they are usually based on the value of the unit, which means the developers recoup much of their capital as soon as the unit is occupied.

An important aspect to consider when entering into a leasehold or licence agreement is how the refund of the money, less DMF if any, is arranged when you vacate the property. Is it refunded to you when you leave, or do you have to wait till the manager finds a new occupier? Does the money you get back contain any element of capital gain and, if so, how is it calculated?

2. **Strata title or group title** which gives you absolute ownership of your unit. You pay for it when you move in, and you sell it, if you can, when you leave.

Strata title provides the perceived security of ownig your own unit but you must understand that it will be just one unit in a village that contains many units as well as facilities such as tennis courts and swimming pools. To run such a centre requires money and skill. This brings up the first big question: Who is going to provide the money and the skill to run the village in which you own a unit?

A strata title complex is run by a body corporate comprising a committee of elected representatives from owners of the individual units. If you have ever been involved in a committee you will be well aware of squabbles and difficulties that can arise when people try to work together. These difficulties may be aggravated when most of the members of the committee are retired with plenty of time on their hands but perhaps little or no commercial experience.

Imagine what may happen if the management of the village is not satisfactory because the body corporate does not do its job properly. Conditions at the village would go from bad to worse, the residents' lives would be nothing but worry and the value of the initial investment in the strata title unit would be greatly reduced.

Now think about it from the developer's point of view. They can do all the work to set up a beautiful development but then find that they are at loggerheads with a body corporate that is often controlled by a handful of people. If conflict between the body corporate and the developers continues, everybody loses.

So, which is best? Lease/licence/company title—or strata/group title? That is something you will have to decide for yourself, for neither is clearly better than the other; both have advantages and disadvantages. As you read on, keep in mind that the most important factors in your decision will be who will manage the village, what will be the ongoing costs and how and when you will recoup your money if you move out. So you can appreciate both sides of the picture, let's now look at it from the developers' point of view.

As the developer sees it

Developers are in business to make a profit and, if they are looking to establish and maintain a thriving business, they will be trying to give the best service possible. This entails building a unit that is value for money, irrespective of the price range, and then providing ongoing service via the management of the village.

The problem with building retirement villages is that they contain far more than just units to live in. There is normally an administration block, security fencing and recreational amenities such as a lounge, pool and tennis court. If serviced apartments are involved, there will also be a central kitchen and laundry facilities. The bigger the complex the more opportunities there are to save money because of economies of scale but, as the complex gets bigger, more capital is required to build it.

Furthermore, if developers build a large retirement village in stages, they have to build many of the common facilities at the start. This places a huge cost burden on the first units sold as they are carrying the bulk of the infrastructure costs for the entire project. Consequently, in the early stages the developer is not making a profit out of those units.

You may now be starting to understand that developers have two choices—build for a quick sale or build for a long-term relationship. If developers want a quick sale, they may have to build the units down to a cost rather than up to a standard. As a result, there have been many instances where developers after a quick dollar have built a shoddy product which looked good on the surface only. They formed the body corporate, sold the units quickly, made their profit, and got out. Four or five years later it is the hapless residents who find the faults in the wiring or the plumbing or in the sealing of the bathrooms and are then faced with the costs of trying to rectify them.

In contrast, those developers who see themselves in the business for the long-term build in the knowledge that they have to maintain the village for maybe 75 years or more. With this is mind they try to provide the best quality that is commensurate with the price they expect to get.

Developers with a long-term attitude realise that if they build a quality product it is virtually impossible to recover their costs in the early stages. They build in the expectation that the good reputation of the village will increase the value of the units in the later stages and they can start making a profit in the fourth or fifth stage.

> **In the next chapter we will look at the costs associated with moving to a retirement village.**

Chapter 8

Retirement village costs

Now let's examine the costs of living in a retirement village. Some of the most important questions are: what are you getting for the money you outlay? what will it cost you each week? what happens when you move out? And always remember: any costs associated with providing you with care or domestic services are normally in addition to the village's fees and charges.

There are four main categories of costs:

1. **Entry cost.** This is the price you pay to gain possession of the unit. This will be either the buying price if it is strata title or company title, or the amount of the interest-free loan you make to the developer if it is a lease or licence arrangement. The amount paid determines homeowner status. If it is less than $135,000 you are a non-homeowner and the amount paid is an assessable asset. If it is above this you are a homeowner and the asset is exempt.
2. **Service charges.** Irrespective of the method of title held, residents are

responsible for the ongoing costs of the village. These include insurance, water rates, general lighting, staff wages, and repairs and maintenance. As these are reimbursable items, the management is not allowed to make a profit on them but can claim only the actual costs. The manager prepares a budget of expenditure for the year and each resident is levied for a proportion of that expenditure.

The method used is similar to that used in body corporates where a unit entitlement is struck that is often based on the floor area of your unit. The use of this formula means that large units pay a higher levy than smaller units and this sometimes causes complaints from residents. For example, they may ask why a unit that is twice as big as another should pay twice the share of such items as the water rates or the salaries of the village staff, when both the small unit and the bigger unit have only two occupants at most.

A simple way of looking at these costs is to compare them with the insurance and maintenance costs of your own home. The situation is also similar to the costs of living in your own home if you decide to leave. You, or your estate, are liable for these ongoing costs until a resale of the unit is finalised.

To protect the rights of the residents, some states now have laws that require developers to refund any fees that have not been used because the budget was overestimated. However, if developers underestimate the fees it is them, and not the residents, who have to make up the shortfall—developers are unable to take a profit out of the service charges.

3. **Internal maintenance.** Naturally residents are responsible for the internal maintenance of their own units and are required to pay for all damage apart from "fair wear and tear". They are also liable for their own electricity and telephone costs as well as insurance of their personal effects. Many villages require outgoing residents to pay the cost of repainting the interior while others will require a complete refurbishment of the unit at the resident's expense and this will be part of the calculation of the departure fee.

4. **Deferred management fee.** This is the cost that causes the most confusion. The deferred management fee (DMF) is also known as a capital replacement fee and in simple terms may be regarded as part of the developer's profit. Many people seem to regard deferred management fees as a "rip-off" but remember, the developers can

make no profit from the service levies or the internal maintenance fees, and often make no profit on the development until they reach the later stages. Certainly, the leasehold or licence fees provide interest-free capital but in the early stages these may not even cover the cost of the infrastructure.

A good definition of a deferred management fee is: "A fee or part of the original purchase price deferred until resale of the residence. It includes operator's remuneration for providing community facilities, return for the financial risk taken to establish the village and delayed payment for part of the purchase price until resale." Yes, that's a fancy way of saying "profit".

From the developer's point of view the great thing about DMFs is that they are payable every time the unit changes hands. However, on average, independent living units resell every nine years and serviced apartments about every four years, so it is clear developers have to be patient.

All the brochures we studied while researching this chapter disclosed the DMF in detail and in simple terms but it is an issue that you should look at carefully so you know exactly what it will cost when you leave the village. Later in the chapter some examples of the way DMF is calculated are listed.

Here are a few examples of actual costs in currently operating retirement villages to show the different way these costs can work.

Village A—with purchase options

This is a highly regarded village run by a public company and offers leasehold title by way of 99-year leases. It has retirement units (referred to as villas) ranging in price from $450,000 to $750,000 and (terrace apartments) serviced apartments priced from $350,000 to $500,000.

The general service fees are $429 per month for the apartments and $610 per month for the villas.

There are four purchase options available:
1. Pay at a fixed price, say $450,000, and pay DMF when you vacate.

2. Pay an additional 10%, say $495,000, and eliminate the DMF. In other words, the developer's profit is being paid up-front.
3. Pay an additional 25%, say $562,500, and pay DMF but have full capital gain.
4. Pay an additional 25% plus 10%, say $607,500, and have no DMF but all capital gain.

Options 1 and 2 give you, or your estate, no capital gain. Options 3 and 4 give you the right to all the capital gain.

Which should you choose? It depends on your pocket and how much you want to leave to your estate. The first option lets you in for the lowest price; the last option gives most to your estate provided, of course, the capital gain is more than the $157,500 you paid to get it. Would you rather have an extra $350,000 to spend now, or is leaving it to your estate more important?

Village B—entry fee and rental (church property)

This is a small retirement village consisting of 16 units run by a church. The purpose of the village is to provide housing to people who are financially disadvantaged. To gain entry to the village a declaration of assets with supporting documentation is required. The amount charged is dependent on the resident's capacity to pay but the village aims to leave the resident with at least $30,000 in financial assets. For example, if the resident has $80,000 worth of assets, $5,000 being a car and $2,000 being personal effects, the village will charge $43,000 as the entry fee.

Occupancy is by way of a loan lease arrangement and the DMF is 15% per year (adjusted proportionately for any partial year) until the earlier of the exhaustion of the loan (approximately 6 years and 9 months) or the date that a new occupant permanently occupies the unit. The residual amount of the loan will be paid 6 months from the date of vacating the unit in the event that a new occupant is not found earlier.

The rental charge is calculated at 30% of the full age pension plus the maximum rent assistance, which equates to $167.50p.w. and the service charge is $38.50p.w.

In the terms of the agreement the owner can provide the resident with 14 days notice requiring the resident to vacate the unit and terminate the agreement if two legally qualified medical practitioners, one of whom is nominated (or agreed to) by the resident and one of whom is nominated by the owner, provide a certificate stating that the resident requires medical or other care of a kind which is not available at the property.

Village C—freehold strata title

This is a quality village set on a huge property offering amenities that include a pool, heated spa, barbecue terrace, bowling greens and a picturesque walking path. Title is freehold strata title and prices start at $389,000 for a one-bedroom unit and $690,000 for a spacious two-bedroom unit. The weekly levy is $145 and DMF is 3% per annum for a maximum of 12 years. Apart from the DMF, the resident keeps all the capital gain on resale. The marketing people for this village claim outgoing residents have received an average capital gain of 5% a year after DMF has been taken off.

They have no restriction on your reselling the unit and you may sell it through local real estate agents or through the village's own marketing division. Most buyers for this village make enquiries at the marketing division and as a result most resales are effected in that way.

Village D—independent living plus aged care

This is a large chain village and offers "living with choices", in this instance 78 independent living apartments and an aged care facility with 52 low care beds and 50 high care beds.

Your buying cost buys you a licence to live in the unit. Two-bedroom units including garages cost $250,000 and the service fees are $110 a week.

The brochure states that the village manager or registered nurse will consult with your doctor and "if one-on-one care is required and appropriate, live in care by personal care assistants can be arranged (on a user pays basis)". The brochure also provides examples of people who have required care from time to time but remained living in the village. The written material advises that if the registered nurse or village manager, in consultation with your doctor, believe that you are at high risk of injury to yourself or others then you will be required to undergo an Aged Care Assessment Team Assessment and move to an appropriate facility without delay but that "very few of our residents ever require a high level of care".

The brochure also hints that residents could move to the next level of care within the complex, but when you read Chapter 15 you will discover that entry to an aged care facility on site is not always that simple.

A schedule of services that are available includes: personal hygiene management (daily), nutrition management, diversional activities, mobility assistance and case management by "Nursing Care Staff". These are provided at a cost of up to $12.50 per half hour between 9am and 5pm Monday to Friday and if required at other times an individual charge is set.

Upon resale the percentage refundable after DMF is worked on a sliding scale but this is conditional upon the unit being reoccupied under a new agreement. The managers claim there is a long waiting list for places and there has never been any difficulty in finding a new occupant.

Village E—rental village only

This village has two types of unit; one bedroom studios and larger one bedroom units where the bedroom and living area are separate. They offer two levels of accommodation: accommodation only and accommodation plus meals. They advise that the studios are only suited to people living on their own while the units are comfortable for a couple. The rental prices for the studios range from $288–$300 per week for accommodation only and $340–$360 per week for the one bedroom units. The prices including meals are $336–$354 per week for a single person in a studio and $450–$480 per week for a couple in a unit.

Village F—aged care only

This village is marketed as "Aged Care with Independence" and has been highly popular. Most rooms are one bedroom apartment-style with some that have adjoining rooms to accommodate couples. Each room on the upper levels has its own balcony, while rooms on the ground floor have private courtyards. Unit prices range from $350,000 to $450,000 and the general service fees are $160 per week.

It is a condition of entry that all residents require care and undergo an assessment from a member of staff who is a Registered Nurse. Each unit has an emergency call button and a health management plan is developed prior to moving in and reviewed regularly by the nurse as part of the service charge.

A price table is provided that details all of the care packages and services that can be provided and the cost associated with each. For example, a package that includes 17.5 hours of care (of which five are provided through a CACP), hot lunch and light dinner daily and an overnight service (where four half hour attendances are provided) is costed at $1,630.25 per week.

The right to occupy is given by a 99-year lease and all care services are provided by the village. The DMF is calculated on the re-sale price and is 10% in the first year, and 6% for the next five years with a maximum of 40%, i.e. after six years with all capital gain given to the resident.

Let's assume you buy one of the apartments on the ground floor so that you can have a small garden to tend to. The entry price is $450,000 and you live in the unit for five years. The re-sale value of your unit is $525,000. The DMF will be calculated as 34%(10+4x6) on $525,000=$178,500 giving you a refund of $346,500 PLUS $75,000 for capital appreciation. The total amount refunded to you will be $421,500.

While the operator intends to look after all residents for as long as they live, they acknowledge that in some circumstances this isn't possible for the health and safety of the resident or other residents of the village.

Chapter 9

Retirement villages—summing up the choices

There is no doubt that retirement village living is fast becoming an attractive option for many retirees and it will be one of Australia's major growth industries as the number of people over 65 increases. The diversity of interests, demand for privacy and space, expectations in terms of additional services, desire for flexible financial arrangements and potential care needs in this age group will make catering to the baby boomers' wants and needs challenging for village operators. In future years village operators may even find themselves acting as virtual aged care providers if their residents are by then accessing the kinds of community care packages we described in Chapter 2. In fact, many village operators already do.

There are hundreds of villages clamouring for your attention, and they offer a wide range of housing options and facilities. As with most things in life, you tend to get what you pay for, but the main factors to think about are what best suits your lifestyle and how much you can afford.

A difficult decision may be choosing between strata title and one of the licence or leasehold arrangements. The initial costs of either option are fairly similar but the main differences may occur in the management of the village and the treatment of the asset when you leave or die. With strata title you own and occupy the unit and, when you die, the unit is passed on to your beneficiaries less any DMF.

In a leasehold retirement village you actually lease your unit on a long-term basis (usually 99 years) and when you die your beneficiaries receive a proportion of the value of the unit less the amount for DMF. Under a loan arrangement you or your estate receive the amount of the loan less DMF.

Usually strata title owners are entitled to any capital gain, but this entitlement may be there with leasehold or licence arrangements if it is set out in the contract documents.

But money is not everything and there are also other important points to consider before deciding on the right choice for you. As we have stressed, the management and maintenance of the village are the key elements in determining how happy you will be living there.

Be aware that with the management of some strata title villages, the developers may, upon the selling of the last unit, move out and leave the management of the village to the residents. In addition, there is the matter of ongoing levies if any facilities need repair. In a strata title complex the body corporate tends to underprovide for future maintenance for fear of creating high unpopular levies. If this happens, the residents have to pay for major repairs as they occur and they can find themselves faced with increasing repair and maintenance costs.

In a leasehold situation the manager stays on. Most leasehold villages have a resident-funded operating arrangement whereby the operating costs of the village are met through a regular fee. The deferred management fee, usually a predetermined percentage of the price of the unit, is paid when the resident leaves the village.

We are aware that some of the information we have given you here may at first seem rather daunting but our intention is to arm you with as much background knowledge as possible to enable you to weigh up each of your options carefully and reach the best decision for your needs. Let us just repeat that, from our personal experience in meeting residents of retirement villages, the vast majority are happy, healthy and contented with their only regret being that they had waited so long to make the move!

SECTION 3

Residential aged care

A great many of us firmly announce that we have no intention of moving into an aged care facility. "An old people's home? Not me!" But the fact is that one third of men and half of all women who reach the age of 65 will at some time live in aged care. And very often when they take the time to investigate their options they are pleasantly surprised.

Many aged care facilities today are more like hotels than the "old age home" of years ago. In fact, it is not uncommon for residents to comment to their children about "what a lovely hotel they are staying in" and "how friendly and helpful the staff are" while on a respite stay in an aged care facility.

The eight chapters in this section look at the various standards and accreditation requirements that govern aged care facilities, some of the special services provided to meet specific needs, and tips to help you find the right facility. We also cover the Assets Assessment process and how the government funds aged care, and examine some of the "small print" of your legal contract with an approved aged care provider. Last but certainly not least in this section, we demystify the varying financial structures involved such as accommodation bonds, accommodation charges, bond retention, the basic daily fee and income tested fees.

We must stress that aged care advice is complex and you may be well advised to seek professional help from a financial planner who specialises in this area. The choices you make about how to fund the cost of care can have wide ranging effects ... on pension entitlement, the cost of care itself, your ability to afford care in the longer term and the amount of money left to your estate. But most importantly, the choice you make should ensure access to the care that is needed.

Chapter 10

Residential aged care—setting the standards

For many elderly people the move to an aged care facility affords them the care they need in a safe, purpose-built environment, with social activities that cater to their age and medical conditions and in some cases are religious or cultural specific.

Predominant among the new aged care facilities are configurations of single rooms with an ensuite to cater to privacy expectations of residents and their families and it is important to be aware that many facilities exceed government requirements in this regard. Government requirements for new aged care facilities are a maximum of two residents per room (with an average across the whole service of no more than 1.5 residents per room), four to every shower or bath and three per toilet. For existing buildings a maximum of four residents per room, six residents per toilet and seven residents per bath or shower is allowed. Exceptions to the number of residents per room can be made where this standard would not be considered culturally appropriate.

Aged care facilities in the past have been referred to as "Hostels" and "Nursing Homes" with many carrying these terms in their name, e.g. Rolling Hills Nursing Home. Hostels provided a low level of care with nursing homes catering to those that had high care needs. A change in care needs, from low to high, would often mean that the resident would need to find and move to a new aged care facility (nursing home). This was obviously unpopular, and difficult for many, and the trend is now to what is called Ageing in Place (AIP) where they remain at the same facility.

The introduction of AIP means that the government allows a resident to remain in a hostel with nursing home care needs and provide the hostel with a higher level of funding (equivalent to that the nursing home would have received) has meant that residents are less likely to need to move from one aged care facility to another.

Most families would agree that moving a loved one into care is something they only want to do once. Similarly residents often form close friendships with other residents, staff and volunteers and don't want to move to a new aged care facility. In doing your research for the appropriate aged care facility, Ageing in Place may be an important consideration, especially if the prospective resident has a condition that is degenerative and this is already known.

Aged care classifications

Nowadays aged care facilities are classified as Low Care, High Care or Extra Services (which is then also distinguished as Low Care or High Care) and it is not uncommon to find more than one type of care, and in some cases all three, under the same roof! As a result, many aged care facilities are able to offer residents choices in the type of care they would like to access. For example, a resident may go to an aged care facility that offers a choice between standard beds and extra service beds. As we will discuss later, a different financial arrangement applies to each of these types of care so it is important to be aware of this and whether or not one may be better suited to you/your family than the other.

It is also becoming more prevalent that, where an accommodation bond is payable, in Low Care or Extra Services, the facility will give the resident options about the amount payable and the way in which it is paid (lump sum or daily fee). These choices can have an impact on your pension entitlement, the ongoing cost of care and exemptions that can be applied to the former home and we'll be looking at this in more detail later.

Bear in mind, too, that within Low Care and High Care (not Extra Services) aged care facilities need to maintain a mixture of residents who pay for themselves and those who are financially disadvantaged (known as Supported Residents) in order for the facility to receive funding from the government.

Many residents and their families have asked us over the years to make recommendations of an aged care facility for them, to which our response has always been "If you had a sore leg would you consult your dentist?" Our expertise is in the financial aspects—we don't know enough about the care side of the business to form a professional opinion.

Of course, we make observations that are probably not dissimilar to those that the family will make: is the facility warm in winter and cool in summer? what do we think of the colour, quality and comfort of the furnishings and the décor? does it smell clean and fresh? (or better yet, of freshly cooked scones!). We also make observations of the staff and whether they are congregating behind the nurse's station, if they appear friendly or stressed and the way in which they engage with the residents and their families. As we all know, the most beautiful furnishings, decor and gardens don't necessarily equate to the best care; it is the staff, (and in many cases the other residents) who will influence the lifestyle someone enjoys within an aged care facility.

Criteria and standards

The decision to build and operate an aged care facility is not one that can be taken lightly.

Residential aged care facilities and the people who work in them are subject to a number of requirements as prescribed by the *Aged Care Act 1997* to ensure the health and safety of the residents.

Before an organisation can provide aged care or receive subsidies from the government, they must apply to the Department of Health and Ageing to become an "Approved Provider". There are key criteria that an approved provider must meet, which include being an incorporated body and being suitable to provide aged care, plus confirming that none of the proposed key personnel is a disqualified individual, convicted of an indictable offence, insolvent or of unsound mind.

In assessing the application the Department will consider the applicant's ability to provide care, their record of financial management, their ability to meet the relevant certification and accreditation standards, and their commitment to the rights of residents. The people named as key personnel (executive decision makers as well as those responsible for the day-to-day operation of the facility) and their history in the provision of aged care services will also play a key role in this process.

Certification

An aged care facility cannot charge an accommodation bond or accommodation charge if the buildings themselves are not certified. Certification looks at:
- Safety and hazards including fire safety and occupational health and safety measures
- Privacy and space including the distribution of beds, toilets, bathrooms and communal areas
- Access and mobility measures such as ramps, grab rails and lifts
- Heating, cooling, lighting and ventilation, as well as security of possessions and perimeters of buildings.

Aged care facilities must also meet state and territory laws (including any local by-laws) in relation to fire safety and in the past have been required to complete a Fire Safety Declaration every year. While they still need to meet the fire safety requirements, they no longer need to confirm this on an annual basis. Aged care facilities are required to inform the Department of Health and Ageing within 28 days of any non-compliance with a law, detailing the extent of the breach and what if any measures have or will be taken and the expected timeframes for this.

Accreditation

An aged care facility must also meet accreditation requirements to be eligible for government funding and this is the responsibility of the Aged Care Standards and Accreditation Agency. Aged care facilities need to undergo a full accreditation prior to the first residents moving in and again within 12 months of the first accreditation. For an existing facility the period of time between an accreditation site audit will vary depending on the facility's history and current level of compliance. A facility meeting all of the outcomes may receive a three-year accreditation while others may receive shorter periods of accreditation. In between audits aged care facilities are subject to regular monitoring. Regardless of the accreditation outcomes every aged care facility will receive at least one unannounced visit from the Aged Care Standards and Accreditation Agency each year.

There are four accreditation standards which cover 44 outcomes that must be met. These standards, listed below, relate to care practices, management of the facility and the staff, the protection of privacy and dignity, and health and safety. As part of the process the Agency's assessors speak with staff as well as residents and their families about the home and how it meets the standards.

Standard 1 relates to the achievement of all the standards. Among other things this standard ensures:
- homes have management and information systems that are responsive to the needs of residents, representatives, staff and stakeholders
- that you have access to a complaints system
- that the staff who care for you are skilled, and
- that the home has the appropriate goods and equipment.

Standard 2 is related to your health and personal care needs and requires that:
- medication is managed safely and correctly
- clinical care meets your needs
- continence is managed effectively
- you are offered a varied, healthy and well-balanced diet

- oral and dental health is maintained, and
- your best level of mobility is achieved.

Standard 3 is about lifestyle and:
- maintaining your independence
- respecting your privacy, dignity and confidentiality
- encouraging your participation in decisions about services the home provides
- fostering your cultural and spiritual life, and
- ensuring residents understand their rights and responsibilities.

Standard 4 requires a safe and comfortable environment that ensures quality of life, your welfare and that of your visitors and the home's staff by:
- minimising fire, security and emergency risks
- having an effective infection control program, and
- providing catering, cleaning and laundry services to enhance your quality of life.

Police checks

Aged Care facilities are responsible for ensuring that their staff and any contractors (including volunteers) likely to have contact with residents of the facility undergo a police check, known as a national criminal history record check. These checks must be renewed every three years. Anyone whose police check confirms that they have been convicted of murder, sexual assault or convicted and imprisoned for any other form of assault cannot work for an aged care service if they are likely to have access to residents. For any other recorded convictions it is at the discretion of the aged care operator to determine whether or not the person is suitable.

Bear in mind that there are many people involved in the running of an aged care facility, some of whom you will see on a regular basis while others you may never see at all.

> *As you can see, there are considerable checks and balances in place these days to ensure that residential aged care facilities are able to offer optimal levels of care in a safe and secure environment.*

Chapter 11

Special services within residential aged care

Cultural and linguistically diverse care

While it is important that people receive the care they need in a safe environment, it is also important that that environment nurture and respect the individual's cultural and linguistic needs. The Australian Government recognises that it is important for people from different cultural or linguistically diverse backgrounds to receive care that meets these needs.

Two programs have been established to assist people in this context: Partners in Culturally Appropriate Care Program and the Community Partners Program. These programs provide information and services to both the care recipient and the aged care provider, helping the latter deliver appropriate care and services. You'll find contact details in the appendix.

To cater to the needs of Aboriginal and Torres Strait Islander communities the government has a number of programs including Multi-Purpose Services located in rural and remote areas and Aboriginal and Torres Strait Islander specific services throughout Australia. The National Aboriginal and Torres Strait Islander Flexible Care Program is designed to provide culturally appropriate care either through a residential or community aged care service. This program operates outside the *Aged Care Act 1997*. Aboriginal and Torres Strait Islanders are also entitled to receive care that respects their cultural diversity through any of the other government funded services, such as Home and Community Care Packages or the National Respite for Carers Program. For more information about the location and types of aged care services for older people from Aboriginal and Torres Strait Islander communities use the contact details in the appendix.

Dementia specific

Some aged care facilities have designated dementia specific areas, generally with keypad doors to prevent residents from wandering. In some cases they employ people who specialise in dementia behaviours to provide advice on how to assist residents in managing their behaviours. Some facilities, for example, have painted certain walls specified colours to help residents find their way back to their room or to a common area. Other facilities have special activities which can include simple things such as making the bed to more co-ordinated activities such as ball games, dancing and exercises to stimulate parts of the brain. Many people with dementia have wandering or repetitive behaviours which is often why it is unsafe for them to remain in their own home. We recently saw a huge dementia specific courtyard that contained a bus stop, post office box and a car to cater to these needs, which was just wonderful!

Multi-Purpose Services

Multi-Purpose Services (MPS) operate in rural and remote communities where the population is not big enough to support the separate services of a hospital, aged care facility and home and community health and aged care services. Multi-Purpose Services can enable people to access a wider range of services than they would otherwise be able to and can allow people who require aged care to stay close to their family and community. While these services are not subject to the same accreditation and standards as an aged care facility, they meet the guidelines of the National Quality Improvement Framework for Multipurpose Services as well as the relevant state or territory health quality framework. It is not necessary to have an ACAT assessment to access services through MPS, although this may be requested as a way of assessing your needs.

Respite provided through a Multi-Purpose Service is not subject to the 63-day limit that applies to respite within a residential aged care facility. In MPS you are able to receive as much respite as the service is able to provide and that you need.

Transitional care

Transitional care is generally short-term care (up to 12 weeks) that is provided to you after a hospital stay and is designed to assist you to continue living in your own home. In some circumstances transitional care is provided to people who are already living in aged care. In these circumstances the aged care facility will continue to receive funding from the government while you are on transitional care leave. Similarly, if prior to your hospital stay you received an aged care package in your own home, such as a Community Aged Care Package, the government will continue to provide funding to the package provider during your absence to ensure your package is available when you return home.

Transitional care can be provided in a hospital, aged care facility, day therapy centre or your own home. The services provided through transitional care can be rehabilitative in nature: speech therapy, occupational therapy, podiatry as well as counselling; and can involve personal care such as assistance with showering, dressing, eating; as well as the provision of transport services to attend appointments.

To be eligible to receive transitional care you will need to have an ACAT assessment while you are still in the hospital and you must complete any other care programs, such as rehabilitation, first.

If you find that you still need the services at the end of your allowable time limit you can request an extension of up to an extra six weeks.

If you receive a transitional care package in your own home you will pay a fee equivalent to 17.5% of the full pension. If the care you receive is in an aged care facility you will pay the same amount as a respite resident which is the Standard Basic Daily Care Fee.

Respite

A really important service for those needing care and for their carers is respite. Respite can be provided in the home, a day care centre or in an aged care facility. In 2009–10 almost 60,000 people received short-term respite care in an aged care facility, equal to almost 1.34 million respite days! Other forms of respite account for 5.1 million hours.

Respite in an aged care facility can last anywhere from a few days to a couple of months. The cost for respite is only the Standard Daily Care Fee ($40.25p.d as at 1 July 2011), no accommodation bond or charge is payable and no income-tested fee applies to respite stays. If you choose to have respite in the extra services category then you will also need to pay the applicable extra service fee.

Respite in an aged care facility can be great way to "try before you buy" or provide a "soft entry" to permanent aged care for people who are frightened about the move. A couple of weeks of respite will give a good indication of what it is like to live in that facility: the activities on offer, the food, and so on. It should also give you time to assess whether you could develop a new network of friends amongst the other residents and enable you to start building relationships with the staff. It is quite common for people to mistake respite as a stay in a hotel—aged care facilities today bear little resemblance to the places your parents may have experienced!

Respite services in your own home are usually shorter term and may consist of just a few hours or an overnight stay to give the carer a break.

Supported Residential Services (Vic & SA)

Not aged care facilities as such, Supported Residential Services—operating in Victoria mostly with a small number in South Australia—offer residential care to people who need assistance with daily activities as well as physical and emotional support. Residents can include people who have a physical disability, people with an intellectual disability or brain injury, people with psychiatric disorders and people with dementia. Many are elderly. Some people live in an SRS for many years, while others are there for a short term or as a result of a disability they have acquired as the result of an accident.

The care services provided vary from one SRS to another and in some cases the service may specify the type of residents it will accept.

SRSs do not receive funding from the Federal or State Government. The State Departments of Health are responsible for registering and monitoring them in accordance with the Health Services Act, as well as dealing with any complaints or non-compliance issues that may arise.

While SRSs are not subject to the same certification and accreditation that applies to Residential Aged Care Facilities, there are legislative guidelines that determine who is eligible to operate an SRS, criteria for carers (including relevant background checks) and the ratio of staff to residents, the way residents' money is handled and the appropriate record keeping, the documentation for detailing costs and care services, as well as the circumstances under which care cannot be provided.

Before you move into an SRS you should obtain a copy of the "Information for Prospective Residents and other Interested Persons" brochure which details the number of people the service cares for, whether they cater to specific care needs, fees and charges, any additional services available and associated costs, and complaint handling procedures.

On entry to an SRS you should receive a Residential Statement and a Care Plan. The Residential Statement will detail the nature of the accommodation (single or shared room) and services you will receive, the fees and charges applicable to you and how and when these are levied and under what circumstances they may change. It will also cover arrangements for temporary leave from the service, reasons why you may be asked to leave and the notice period that will apply, plus "house rules" around such things as behaviour, use of common areas, smoking and the consumption of alcohol.

Note that the fees and charges related to an SRS are not regulated and can vary enormously. Some charge a weekly fee calculated as a percentage of the full pension (and in some cases rent assistance)—for example, 85% of the full pension and government rent assistance (approximately $350p.w.). Other SRS facilities set a market price fee and $1,000p.w. or more is not unheard of.

The Care Plan will normally be developed between yourself (or your advocate) and the personal care co-ordinator at the SRS. If he/she thinks it is necessary, they may ask your permission to discuss your care needs with your family, your doctor or other medical professionals. The care plan will detail your care needs and the services that will be provided to meet those needs. The care plan will normally set a date for review not greater than 12 months' time although you may undertake an earlier review if you wish and/or your care needs change..

The personal care co-ordinator (PCC) is responsible for the co-ordination of care for all residents and must have a minimum qualification of Certificate III in Community Services (Aged Care). The PCC may assist you to access other services that are not provided by the SRS such as transport to medical appointments, attendance at a day therapy centre, nursing services and social support. If you wish to access these services through Veteran's Home Care or a Community Aged Care Package, you will need to have an ACAT assessment. If you access the services through Home and Community Care packages, HACC undertakes the assessment. Where services are provided by your SRS, however, such as meals, domestic assistance or personal care such as assistance with showering etc., you cannot opt to access them via the government packages.

> *It's confusing we know BUT the Supported Residential Services (Vic & SA) are not the same as the Supported Residents classification (fully supported and partially supported) that we describe in Chapter 14.*

Chapter 12
Finding the right aged care facility

There are two ways to manage the process of finding an aged care facility: using a placement consultant or doing it yourself. We'll examine both later in this chapter but first let's look at some factors that you will need to consider in determining exactly what you are looking for in an aged care facility.

Level of care

In determining which facility will be appropriate, the first step is to determine the level of care required: low care or high care. If you already have an ACAT assessment this step has been done. If not, you will need to wait for this to be carried out.

In some cases a doctor, nurse or other medical professional may give you an indication of what they expect the result of the ACAT to be and this could assist you in starting your search while the formal process is being undertaken. Bear in mind, however, that they cannot guarantee this will be the actual outcome of the assessment. Don't make any firm decisions until you have your written ACAT report.

Once you know the level of care required, you will need to consider whether or not you want extra services. Often this is a difficult decision to make without seeing actual facilities and being able to make a comparison so your thinking should probably be more along the lines of whether or not you will consider an extra service facility in order to have a higher level of accommodation or services available.

While it is crucial to know the level of care you or your loved one requires, it will also be important to know the level of care of the other residents and how this might affect day-to-day life in the facility. Aged care facilities can cater to a diverse range of care needs and, if many residents are in the high care category, you may need to think very carefully about whether you or your loved one will "fit in".

For example, many low care facilities offer Ageing in Place and, while that means that new residents are classified as low care, it doesn't mean that everyone living there remains low care. If the facility has been operating for a number of years it is likely that a proportion of the residents will now be high care. So while you may think that a low care facility with Ageing in Place sounds a good option for your current low care needs, a facility where the majority of residents have become high care may not be the best environment.

Geographic location

This is probably one of the biggest considerations, particularly if the person moving into care currently lives some distance away. Families are often faced with the difficult decision of finding care close to the person's existing home so that they remain in their community and near friends, or moving them closer to people willing to take some responsibility for them. It can be an incredibly difficult decision.

Geographical location is also crucial in facilitating visiting when one partner is moving into care but one is remaining at home, especially if driving has become difficult or is no longer possible.

Interests/activities

Finding a facility that provides activities or caters to the interests of the person moving in can play a much bigger role than many family members think. While many facilities offer outings and in some cases transport services, there will often come a time when the person's care needs mean that they can only participate in activities that are within the facility. These activities serve a number of very important functions that may not at first be obvious. They create an opportunity for social interaction with other residents, staff and volunteers, they stimulate creativity and are often a time of reminiscence, recalling the mother or other family member or friend teaching them the craft. Most importantly, these activities give the resident something to look forward to and can assist in reducing depression. Many facilities offer diversional therapy services such as musical sessions, visits with animals, planting flowers and vegetable gardens.

Waiting list and interim care

While there may be many aged care facilities in your chosen area, that doesn't mean there will be a bed in the facility of your choice.

When someone is moving from hospital to aged care, the family will often be asked to provide a list of five or six facilities within a few days, with the first facility to accept the resident being the one they go to. Obviously, it is crucial to have done your homework and ensure that you feel comfortable with the facilities you have nominated. Moving from a hospital will give you a higher level of priority than other people on the waiting list and you should use this to your advantage.

For people who are moving from a home environment it may be necessary to seek interim care, either through respite or the delivery of care packages into the home. Once you have determined the facility or a short list that you are happy with, you will need to make an application for admission. Some facilities have their own paperwork while others use the government forms. All facilities will need a copy of the Aged Care Client Record (from the ACAT Assessment).

Waiting times for admission will vary from one facility to another. Often it depends on the type of resident the facility needs to admit next to manage their resident mix of supported residents and non-supported residents.

In most cases the application will require the disclosure of the prospective resident's assets or a copy of the asset assessment so that the facility knows what type of resident they are admitting. Obviously this can also create discrimination where a bond is payable for residents with a greater capacity to pay. You should always make an honest declaration. When a bed becomes available, you need to be ready to move—it is not uncommon for a resident to leave and a new resident to enter (even if it is on pre-entry leave) on the same day! (Pre-entry leave is explained in Chapter 15.)

While you are waiting for acceptance you should determine what is going to be taken to the aged care facility in terms of clothing, toiletries and personal effects (photographs and trinkets that are important to you). You should ensure that any valuable items taken are insured. It is not uncommon for residents to misplace things and keeping large sums of cash is not advisable. You also need to label all the clothing that is being taken. This can be done with a permanent marker or with name tags that you can iron or sew on.

The do-it-yourself approach to finding a facility

There are a lot of resources available to you if you have the time and energy to dedicate to a DIY search.

www.agedcareonline.com.au or www.agedcareguide.com.au will provide you with information about the type of care the facility provides: low care, high care, extra services, and the number of beds for each type of care. They will also provide you with information about whether the facility caters to people with certain cultural or linguistic needs; for example, the facility may cater to people who are Chinese and have staff who speak the languages, and the food and activities will be oriented towards people who share this background.

In some instances the facilities may use these websites to advertise vacancies.

Using a placement agent/broker/consultant

Aged Care Placement Consultants have extensive knowledge of the industry and of all types of facilities. A good consultant will be able to help you make the right choice based on the criteria that matter to the resident and the family. Information regarding the cost of care will also be provided. Concerns regarding the types and level of care and the ability of the facilities to manage the care needs of the potential resident are addressed and any questions answered.

Other considerations which affect the decision making process include geographic implications, time restraints, cultural and religious appropriateness, environment—both general (gardens, aspect and view) and specific (room type & size, fixtures and fittings etc), as well as current accreditation status.

A placement consultant will talk you through all of these issues in order to guide you to the best possible options for care. Their job is to help alleviate the stress and confusion surrounding the move into aged care. Your expectation for the service you employ should be that the process is easier than DIY, the information is correct and up to date, and that the primary concern of your consultant is to achieve the best possible care outcome for you and your family.

It is important to have an open and honest relationship with your consultant and you in turn must feel that the consultancy is transparent and compassionate towards your needs.

In choosing a consultant look for these factors:
- an open and honest manner
- a holistic approach to the process of providing options for care
- genuine concern about the outcome of the process i.e. finding the most appropriate facility or care option
- good communication and regular feedback
- accessibility, someone to talk to who will answer your ongoing questions

- fee transparency, keeping in mind that fees can vary from $500 to $2500
- extensive experience in placement consulting and up-to-date knowledge
- independence i.e. not being paid by facilities to fill beds. With a "client pays" model, the consultant is working for your best interests only
- reputation within the industry—the ability to secure the most appropriate place is often based on the relationship the consultant has with the facilities the client is interested in
- knowledge about all the options for aged care, not just residential options
- the ability to help you formulate a plan for future care. This may include accessing resources which would enable someone to stay in their home for as long as possible, downsizing options such as retirement living or serviced apartment living, and in home care and respite
- the ability to explain fully and succinctly the process of going into aged care relevant to your particular situation
- follow up with the family and the facility to ensure all is well and answer any further questions.

By using a reputable placement consultant you gain the experience of an informed, knowledgeable, independent person who should be able to assist you with all your concerns regarding the transition into aged care. Their job is to ensure that all the statutory requirements are met including completing and submitting the relevant paperwork, liaising with the relevant case managers, social workers and medical staff, researching the facilities that meet your requirements, submitting applications to those you are interested in and acting as advocate for you with the facility. This can represent invaluable support during a difficult time.

Be aware, however, that some organisations call themselves placement consultants when they are essentially bed brokers or bed fillers. They are driven by placing residents into the next available bed as opposed to matching the potential resident's care needs with the most appropriate facility. While the service they offer may suit some, there is a risk of inappropriate placement. If this happens, it is of course possible to move between facilities but this can be extremely disruptive for the resident. As anyone who has moved a loved one into aged care will tell you, it can be an incredibly emotional process—it is not something you want to do twice if it can be avoided.

As in every service industry, there are disreputable operators within the placement field. Facilities and larger care organisations will often choose not to work with so-called placement consultancies who limit the options for the client.

Unfortunately it can be difficult to determine who is and who is not reputable. Word of mouth is the best referee. Ask around for information on placement agencies from people you know. If by chance you strike an agency that does not meet your expectations or does not do what they say they will, don't be afraid to end the contact and find another.

> ***Don't forget:***
> Before you can access an aged care facility, you will need to have an ACAT Assessment. See Chapter 3.

Of course, at the same time as you are trying to manage all of these factors, you will also need to be aware of the different financial arrangements at each of the facilities and how these fit with your situation. In the next chapter we examine how your assets might be assessed to determine the amount you pay for accommodation costs in an aged care facility.

Chapter 13
The assets assessment process

In addition to an ACAT Assessment, there is another assessment process you may have to go through before entering aged care—an Assets Assessment.

Unlike ACAT, the assets assessment is not compulsory unless you want to claim supported resident status. You will find, however, that some aged care facilities prefer new potential residents to have an assessment.

Understanding the outcome of the assets assessment for aged care prior to completing it is crucial. We cannot stress this too highly. In some cases, for example, you could be assessed as capable of paying a higher bond than a particular aged care facility is asking and so you would be better advised to avoid the assets assessment and negotiate directly with the facility. You should also be aware that the timing of this assessment for couples can create very different outcomes. We will explore some of these possible outcomes later in this chapter.

You undertake your part of this process by completing a Request for Assets Assessment form (it's generally known as the blue book). The information you supply is used to determine your assessable assets—so that the maximum amount you can be asked to pay in the form of accommodation bond or accommodation charge can be calculated.

Your assessable assets for aged care are often different to your assessable assets for pension purposes. That's because, unless certain criteria are met, your home is included in your assessable assets.

Generally speaking, your assessable assets for aged care are any asset in Australia or overseas that you have a financial interest in, including property, investments and non-financial assets such as your car, contents, collections, artwork etc. If you are a member of a couple (including same sex couples) half of the total assets will be considered to belong to you.

What's included and what's not

Gifts

Since the budget of 10 May 2006 people entering aged care after 1 January 2007 who gift in excess of $10,000 in a single financial year and $30,000 in a five-year period will have those assets included in the assessable assets for aged care purposes. These assets will be assessable for determining the amount of accommodation payment (bond or charge) you can be asked to pay and your eligibility to be a supported resident.

The deemed income will be included in the calculation of your income tested fee.

The asset and income are also assessable for the calculation of pension entitlement.

Superannuation

The value of assets held in a superannuation fund forms part of the assessable assets for aged care if you have met a condition of release under SIS legislation—the Superannuation Industry (Supervision) Act. While most people living in aged care will meet a condition of release, either due to age or the fact that they are unable to return to employment due to their disabilities, their partner may not. In this case the value of the partner's superannuation would not form part of the assessable assets.

Complying income streams

Complying income streams purchased prior to 20 September 2007 that had a 50% or 100% asset test exemption for pension purposes are 100% exempt from the calculation of aged care assets. Income streams with a full or partial asset test exemption that are voluntarily rolled over after 20 September 2007 will generally become fully asset tested.

Farms

If your principal place of residence—your home—is a farm it is important to be aware of the assets assessment for rural homeowners. As a general rule, your home and the land surrounding your home (the first two hectares) is considered your home, with any land in excess considered to be curtilage (even if it is on the same title as your home and the first two hectares). (Curtilage is just a legal term for the land surrounding a property.) The curtilage is considered an assessable asset for for both aged care and pension purposes unless you meet the following criteria:
- You or your partner are of Age Pension age and receive (or are eligible to receive) an Age Pension or Carer Payment from

Centrelink or a Service Pension from the Department of Veteran's Affairs
- You or your partner have lived in the property continuously for the past 20 years AND
- You or your partner satisfy the extended land use test by making effective use of any productive land to generate an income (given your capacity to do so).

The extended land use test doesn't mean that you or your partner must work the land personally, but it does consider whether the land is being used productively to generate an income if this is possible. The extended land use test can be applied if a family member is farming the land or if you are leasing the land to a third party (for a commercial rate) and they are farming the land. Similarly, if the land has limited or no potential commercial use this will be considered. For people in an Exceptional Circumstances drought affected area the effective land use test will automatically be applied while the Exceptional Circumstances exist.

Your home

Your home will be exempt if (at the date of the assessment):
- Your partner or a dependent child is living there

- A carer who is eligible to receive an income support payment has been living there for the past two years
- A close relative who is eligible to receive an income support payment has been living there for the past five years.

> *It is important to be aware that Carer's Allowance is not considered to be an Income Support Payment. Income Support Payments include pensions and benefits paid by Centrelink such as Age Pension, Disability Pension, Carer's Pension and Newstart Allowance, as well as age and service pensions and income support supplements paid by the Department of Veterans' Affairs.*

So, Centrelink doesn't consider Carer's Allowance as income support.

I wonder if many carers do either?

Staying up to date

When completing the Request for Assets Assessment Booklet for aged care you are given the option of providing all the details of your assets or of providing just the details of your living arrangements and the value of these and leaving all other assets to be assessed on the basis of details you previously provided to Centrelink or the DVA. If you opt for the latter option, make sure you check what details are on file prior to ticking this box as it is not uncommon for these records to be out of date.

The assessable assets formula

The formula used to calculate the maximum amount of accommodation bond or accommodation charge you can be asked to pay is quite straightforward. It's your total assessable assets minus the minimum assets amount (currently $39,000).

For example, if your total assessable assets are determined to be $510,000, then the maximum accommodation bond you can be asked to pay is $510,000−$39,000=$471,000. The maximum accommodation charge you can be asked to pay is currently capped at $30.55 per day and applies to people with assessable assets above $102,544. Therefore if your assessable assets are $510,000, you can still only pay a maximum accommodation charge of $30.55 per day.

For couples

If you are a couple, the assessable assets are considered on a 50/50 basis, irrespective of in whose name the asset is held, and the minimum assets amount ($39,000) is deducted from each share.

The timing of an asset assessment can create very different outcomes when dealing with a couple.
• A couple who both enter care on the same day and submit to the asset assessment after they enter will each have 50% of the value of the former home assessed in their assets.
• A couple who enter care on separate days and submit their assets assessment on or after entry to care will have the value of the home exempted from the first to enter and half assessed against the second.
• A couple who both complete the assets assessment prior to entering care will both declare that the spouse lives in the home, thereby exempting the home from each in the assets assessment.

Case Study

Jack and Shirley are full pensioners and have recently been assessed as requiring care. Jack requires high care, while Shirley requires low care. The Aged Care Assessment Team has pro-vided them with a number of documents to

read and complete, including the "Request for an Assets Assessment" from the Department of Health and Ageing.

Jack and Shirley's assets are:

Home	$600,000
Bank Accounts	$5,000
Term Deposits	$50,000
Car	$5,000
Contents	$5,000

Assessed while both living at home:

If Jack and Shirley complete the asset assessment today, while both of them are still living at home (or while one is in hospital or respite care), they would each declare that the other is still living in the home and their assessable assets would be:

$65,000 ÷ 2 = $32,500 each less $39,000 = $0 (−$6,500) each

The asset assessment would show that both Shirley and Jack have assessable assets of less than the minimum assets amount of $39,000 each. Shirley could not be asked to pay an accommodation bond and Jack could not be asked to pay an accommodation charge, and they would both be classified as Fully Supported Residents.

Assessed on or after entering care on separate days:

If Jack and Shirley entered care on separate days, with Jack entering first and Shirley entering second, with the asset assessment completed on or after they each entered care, Jack's assessable assets would be considered to be less than $39,000 (because on the day he entered Shirley was still living in the home) and he would be classified as a Fully Supported Resident, while Shirley's assessable assets would be:

$300,000 (half the house)+$32,500 (half the assets outside the house) less $39,000=$293,500 which would be the maximum accommodation bond Shirley could be asked to pay.

If we flip the order and Shirley enters first and Jack enters second then the assessable assets would be reversed, Shirley would have less than $39,000, would be classified as a Fully Supported Resident and would not pay an accommodation bond and Jack's assessable assets would be $293,500 and he would pay an accommodation charge of $30.55 per day.

Assessed on or after entering care together:

If Jack and Shirley both entered care on the same day and completed their asset assessment on or after they entered care, their assessable assets would be:

$300,000 (half the house)+$32,500 (half the assets outside the house) less $39,000=$293,500 each.

In this case neither would be eligible to be a Fully Supported Resident. Shirley could be asked to pay an accommodation bond of up to $293,500 and Jack's accommodation charge would be $30.55 per day.

While it may seem that the best option is the first scenario, where neither Jack nor Shirley need to pay an accommodation payment, this may have adverse effects further down the track. It could, for example, limit their ability to access care, negatively impact on their future pension entitlement and restrict their options in terms of the way in which they fund their care.

We examine some of these implications in the Case Studies you'll find in Section 4 of this book.

Chapter 14

How the government funds aged care & supported residents

While many aged care facilities may refer to themselves as a "private" facility, the majority of aged care facilities are funded by the government through the Aged Care Funding Instrument (ACFI).

ACFI replaced the RCS (Resident Classification System) in March 2008. The RCS had 8 classifications of resident care needs (RCS 1–8): low care—residents with an RCS classification of 5-8, high care—residents with an RCS of 1–4. ACFI was introduced to provide funding that better matched a person's care needs, with 64 possible computations of care classification.

Today a resident's care needs are classified as either Nil, Low, Medium or High in three categories: Activities of Daily Living, Behaviours and Complex Healthcare.

Activities of Daily Living cover nutrition, mobility, personal hygiene, toileting and continence.

Behaviour covers cognitive skills, wandering, verbal behaviour, physical behaviour and depression.

Complex Healthcare looks at medication and complex healthcare.

The amount of ACFI paid to an aged care facility will be calculated by adding the amount payable in each domain, as per the table on page "Daily ACFI subsidy rates (1 July 2011–30 June 2012)" on page 77. For example, $30.90+$0.00+$13.90 per day for a resident with a low care ACAT whose care needs are classified as Low in Activities of Daily Living, Nil in Behaviours and Low in Complex Healthcare. From 1 July 2011 there is no cap on the ACFI.

Daily ACFI subsidy rates (1 July 2011–30 June 2012)

	Activities of Daily Living (ADL)	Behaviour Supplement (BEH)	Complex Health Care Supplement (CHC)
Nil	$0.00	$0.00	$0.00
Low	$30.90	$7.06	$13.90
Medium	$67.28	$14.63	$39.60
High	$93.21	$30.82	$57.18

Once a person moves into aged care ACFI is used to determine if their care needs are low or high. A person whose care needs are classified as High in ADL's, Behaviours or CHC with a score above Nil in any of the other categories or who has care needs of medium or high in two out of three domains is classified as a high care resident. Residents with care needs below these levels are classified as low care.

Financial supplements

In addition to ACFI aged care facilities can receive financial supplements to cover residents with needs such as oxygen and enteral feeding.

Understanding how aged care facilities receive funding from the government can assist you in understanding the financial viability of some residents. For example, a resident who is classified as Nil, Low, Nil and is fully supported would represent to a facility a maximum of $40.25 (daily care fee paid by the resident)+$30.55 (supported resident supplement)+$7.06 (ACFI) which may be insufficient to cover the cost of providing accommodation, meals, laundry and personal care.

The daily income tested fee paid by a resident is used by the government to offset the funding (ACFI) provided to the facility for that resident on a dollar for dollar basis.

Supported residents (formerly known as concessional and assisted residents)

A common misconception about aged care facilities is that if you don't have any money, you won't get in. In reality, if you don't have any money, you may stand a better chance than someone with some money.

As we pointed out in Chapter 10, in order to receive funding from the government, aged care facilities need to maintain a mix of residents who pay for themselves and those who are financially disadvantaged. The government sets the mix on a regional basis, known as the supported resident ratio, taking into account the socio-economic demographics of the area. The ratios range between 16% and 40%, with the major capital cities being at the lower end of the scale and regional and rural areas being at the upper end of the scale. For example, Brisbane North, Melbourne Eastern Metro, Northern Sydney and South Australia's Yorke, Lower North and Barossa all have ratios around 16%, while Alice Springs, Kimberly and Pilbara all have a ratio of 40%.

Facilities that don't meet their ratio can have their funding affected or sanctions imposed by the government. Facilities that keep a ratio of 40% or more receive maximum funding from the government, while those who maintain a ratio below 40% receive funding at 75% of the maximum. Currently the maximum funding for a supported resident is equal to the accommodation charge ($30.55 per day).

There are two types of supported resident: fully supported and partially supported (formerly Concessional and Assisted Residents). Fully supported residents have assessable assets less than the minimum assets amount (currently $39,000), while partially supported residents have assets greater than the minimum but less than the upper assets threshold (currently $102,544).

Fully supported residents cannot be asked to pay an accommodation bond or an accommodation charge. Partially supported residents pay a calculated amount of accommodation bond or charge.

The maximum accommodation bond is simply the total assessable assets minus the minimum assets amount. For example, if the total assessable assets are $80,000, the maximum accommodation bond payable would be $80,000 less $39,000=$41,000.

The accommodation charge is calculated at $1 per day for every $2,080 of assessable assets above $39,000. For example, if the assessable assets were $80,000, the accommodation charge would be $41,000÷$2,080=$19.71 per day.

In the above example, if the facility were maintaining a ratio of 40% or more, the amount of supplement paid would be $10.84 per day (maximum accommodation charge of $30.55 less $19.71 actually received), whereas if the facility were maintaining a ratio of less than 40% the supplement would be $3.20 per day (75% of $30.55 less $19.71).

Financial hardship

Financial hardship is not the same as being a supported resident. Financial hardship provisions enable residents to receive financial assistance with ongoing costs when they are genuinely unable to meet these obligations.

For example, when applying for financial hardship you can apply for assistance with your daily care fee or income-tested fee; assistance in meeting the accommodation bond or charge; or respite care costs.

In assessing your application for financial hardship the Department of Health and Ageing will look at your asset and income position and will only consider financial hardship applications where assets or income are truly unrealisable. If assets are being retained for other reasons, such as the maintaining of assets for beneficiaries, this will not be considered grounds for financial hardship. Likewise, application for financial hardship due to the assessment of assets that have been gifted in the last five years will not be considered.

Chapter 15

Your legal contract for aged care

Residential Care Agreement

The Residential Care Agreement (RCA) is a legal contract between you (or the person receiving care) and the care provider. The Residential Care Agreement sets out your rights and responsibilities as a resident as well as the rights and responsibilities of the aged care facility in delivering care and other services to you.

There are two types of RCA: for respite residents and for permanent residents.

The respite RCA will set out:
- The date on which your stay begins and ends
- The type of care you will be provided—low care, high care or extra services
- If extra services are being provided, the details of the extra services.

As a respite resident you pay no accommodation bond or charge and an income tested fee will not be applied either. Most respite residents only pay the standard rate of daily care fee ($40.25). Those who choose to have respite in an extra services facility will need to pay the applicable extra service fee.

The permanent RCA will state:
- The date of permanent entry
- The type of care you will be provided—low care, high care or extra services—and the details of what is included, such as furniture, linen, cleaning and laundry services, toiletries etc, as well as medical equipment such as walkers and wheelchairs, etc.
- The details of extra services if provided; for example, a single room with ensuite, daily newspaper, beer, wine or champagne with dinner, hairdressing, massage therapies etc.
- The financial arrangements that will apply to you—the amount of accommodation bond and method of payment (lump sum, periodic payment or combination); if the bond is not paid in full, the interest rate applicable; the amount of retention that will be deducted from the bond or included in the periodic payment; or the amount of accommodation charge
- If you are a supported resident, confirmation that you will not be paying an accommodation bond or charge (fully supported) or confirmation that you will be paying a calculated amount (partially supported)

- The daily care fee and income tested fee that will apply until the Department of Health and Ageing provides these amounts (these are often referred to as the "initial" or "interim" fees)
- The amount of any extra service fee
- The method of payment and when it is payable—normally a direct debit or electronic funds transfer for the daily amount multiplied by the number of days in the month and payable in advance.

The Residential Care Agreement will need to be signed within 21 days of entering the facility and can be signed by the resident or their Legal Personal Representative. There is a 14-day cooling off period which means you can advise the aged care facility within 14 days of signing that you wish to terminate the agreement. In this case, you will need to pay any fees and charges for the period of your stay and any overpayment or lump sum accommodation bond will be refunded to you when you leave or at the end of the 14-day period.

Taking leave

If you wish to take a holiday or spend the night or weekend with family or friends you are entitled to do so. You should discuss your absence with the manager of your aged care facility and let them know when you will be leaving and returning. This type of leave is called social leave and you are entitled to a maximum of 52 nights per year. While you are absent you will need to continue paying your fees and charges. If you wish to be absent for more than 52 nights you may find that the facility will require you to pay an additional sum as the government subsidies will not be paid to them for a longer period of absence. It is not uncommon for the Residential Care Agreement to stipulate that any absences in excess of the allowed time will mean that you need to pay both your care fees and the amount of funding that the government would pay if you were not absent.

Some people secure their place in a facility by paying the necessary charges but choose to take a few days' leave prior to entering to sort out matters and prepare for the move. This is known as pre-entry leave. Preentry leave can be taken for a maximum of seven days prior to entering aged care and is counted as part of the 52 days social leave.

Leaving care to attend hospital is not counted within the social leave limit.

Moving facilities—the costs

At some point you may wish or need to move from one aged care facility to another. Such a move is a little more complex than moving from your own home as there are rules around what the new aged care facility can charge you, depending on what you paid at the original facility.

If you have paid an accommodation bond to the first home and the second home is willing and able to accept this, then you can agree to have the balance of your accommodation bond transferred to them. The accommodation bond balance is the amount you paid to the first facility minus any retention amounts or other fees and charges that were outstanding when you left. Your new aged care facility can only charge the balance of the retention payments. For example, if you lived in the first aged care facility for two years, the next aged care facility can only charge retention for a maximum of three years. If you lived in the first facility for more than five years, the second facility could not deduct any retention from your bond.

If you have paid an accommodation bond to the first facility but the second facility is not willing or cannot accept the bond, the balance will be refunded to you. Some high care facilities cannot accept bond payments. In this case you will need to pay an accommodation charge to the new facility. The amount will be based on your assessable assets at the time you move.

If you were paying an accommodation charge in the first facility and the second facility also operates on this system, the amount you will pay will be the same. However, if you believe your assessable assets are less than they were when you first entered the original facility or if you entered the first facility without undertaking an asset assessment, you may wish to consider a new asset assessment as this could result in a lower accommodation charge.

While many government documents will tell you that you cannot pay a bigger bond to the new facility than you paid to the old one, the reality of this is a little different.

In the past the amount of accommodation bond was often the amount set by the government as the "pensioner allowed" amount. By paying this amount the resident (if a pensioner) was entitled to pay the daily care fee at the pensioner rate and the facility received a pensioner supplement. The accommodation bond amount was set at a maximum of 10 times the single basic pension. For example, in April 2006 the pensioner allowable limit for accommodation bonds was $137,500. If that bond was transferred to a new facility today the balance would be only $121,570 (less any unpaid fees and charges) and it is unlikely that the new facility would accept this amount.

Similarly, a high care facility with the choice of refunding the balance of the bond and instead receiving $30.55 per day ($11,150.75p.a.) as an accommodation charge may well prefer that option.

Bond prices have increased significantly over the last five years. In 2004–5 the total value of bonds held in Australia was $4.3bn; in 2008-9 this amount was $9.1bn. During that period extra services have also become more prevalent.

If a resident of an existing facility wishes to move to a higher level of accommodation or services within that facility, they may find the accommodation bond they have paid to be insufficient. In such cases the facility and the resident can negotiate a new bond amount but this cannot exceed the assessable assets minus the minimum assets amount (i.e. the maximum accommodation bond allowed to be charged) as at the date of permanent entry to the facility.

A resident can only ever pay one bond, but in some cicumstances can top up an existing bond. Any new bond amount will need to be advised to the Department of Health and Ageing and Centrelink/DVA.

For a resident who is moving from one facility to another the same rules apply. However, the transfer of the bond balance will be the applicable bond amount at the date of entry to the new facility with the new bond amount being negotiated thereafter. To provide certainty to both parties (for the resident how much they will be asked to pay and for the facility how much will be paid) negotiations for the new bond are normally done prior to the resident moving.

What if you have a complaint?

If you have a complaint about the care or services you are receiving (or not receiving!) you should first raise your concerns with the Facility Manager/Director of Nursing. If you don't feel that the facility is working with you to resolve the issue or the issue is very serious, you should lodge a complaint with the Aged Care Complaints Investigation Scheme (known as CIS). CIS is a free service which has the powers to investigate concerns about care and services from approved providers, whether delivered through a community package or within an aged care facility. Where necessary, CIS can take action or refer the matter to other appropriate organisations such as nursing and medical registration boards or the police.

You can contact CIS directly by telephone, mail or via the Department of Health and Ageing's website—refer to the appendix for details. Alternatively, you may wish to contact an advocacy service to assist you. Advocacy services operate in all states and territories and will inform you of your rights and assist with lodging your complaint.

You have the right to privacy and even anonymity in relation to the information you provide. If CIS needs to disclose your personal information—for example, to refer the matter to another organisation—they will inform you first. If you have any concerns about the handling of your information you should discuss these with a CIS manager. If you are still unhappy you can raise the issue with the Office of the Aged Care Commissioner or the Office of the Privacy Commissioner, contact details are available in the appendix.

Chapter 16
Accommodation bonds, charges & retention

Remember what we've been telling you—a different financial arrangement applies to each of the three types of care available in aged care facilities. And that some facilities will offer only one type of care but others may have more than one—and perhaps all three—under one roof. In this chapter we examine how these financial arrangements work.

Low Care

Financial structure

Accommodation bond+daily care fee+income tested fee

Low Care aged care facilities provide assistance to those with a Low Care ACAT in the form of meals, laundry and low level nursing care. Low Care facilities also often provide Respite (see Chapter 11 for details of respite care).

The accommodation bond is a sum paid on entry (as lump sum or periodic payment) from which the facility is entitled to take monthly retention amounts and any fees and charges. A little further on in this chapter we describe how accommodation bonds are applied.

High Care

Financial structure

Daily care fee+accommodation charge+income tested fee

The accommodation charge is the daily accommodation payment for people who enter a high care facility (in lieu of an accommodation bond). The amount of accommodation charge is set as at the date of permanent entry and based on your assessable assets. Like many of the other aged care fees and charges, the accommodation charge has undergone some significant changes in recent years (as shown in the table below).

Residents who entered prior to 1 July 2004 will only pay an accommodation charge for up to five years.

Maximum accommodation charge

Residents who entered care between	All non-supported residents	Non-pensioners	Pensioners
20 Mar 2011–19 Sep 2011	$30.55		

20 Sep 2010–19 Mar 2011	$28.72		
20 Mar 2010–19 Sep 2010	$26.88		
20 Sep 2009–19 Mar 2010		$26.88	$25.02
20 Mar 2009–19 Sep 2009		$26.88	$23.22
20 Sep 2008–19 Mar 2009		$26.88	$21.39
20 Mar 2008–19 Sep 2008		$26.88	$19.56
1 Jul 2007–20 Mar 2008	$17.55		
1 Jul 2006–30 Jun 2007	$17.13		
1 Jul 2005–30 Jun 2006	$16.63		
1 Jul 2004–30 Jun 2005	$16.25		

A resident can agree with an aged care facility to defer payment of the accommodation charge for a period of time or have it paid from their estate. In these circumstances the aged care facility can charge interest on the unpaid accommodation charge. The interest charged on an unpaid accommodation charge is different to the interest charged on unpaid accommodation bonds. The interest on an unpaid accommodation charge can be no more than twice the lowest deeming rate that applied at the date of entry. For a person entering care after 20 March 2010 this would be 6%(2x3%).

Interest on unpaid accommodation charge

Residents who entered care between	Maximum permissible interest rate
20 Mar 2010–19 Sep 2011	6%
20 Mar 2009–19 Mar 2010	4%
17 Nov 2008–19 Mar 2009	6%
20 Mar 2008–16 Nov 2008	8%
20 Mar 2007–19 Mar 2008	7%
20 Mar 2004–19 Mar 2007	6%

Extra services (Low Care or High Care)

Financial structure

Accommodation bond+daily care fee+extra service fee+income tested fee

Aged care facilities can apply for extra service status for all or a designated part of their facility. Extra services are defined as "hotel" type services, which can include higher standards of accommodation and increased entertainment and food choices. However, the provision of these services must be "significantly higher than average" to be granted extra service status. Residents who choose to live in an extra service facility will need to pay an accommodation bond (irrespective of whether they are low care or high care) and will be charged a Daily Extra Service Fee which is approved by the government and varies from one facility to another depending on the type of extra services being provided.

Extra Service Facilities are not required to maintain a ratio of Supported Residents and do not receive accommodation supplements from the government for Supported Residents.

Accommodation bond

An accommodation bond is the accommodation payment for low care and extra service residents whose assets exceed the minimum assets amount (currently $39,000). Residents whose assessable assets are less than this amount don't pay an accommodation bond and are recognised as "Fully Supported Residents"—refer to Supported Residents in Chapter 14.

Since 1 July 2005 accommodation bonds have been an exempt asset for pension purposes and the amount of accommodation bond paid is not a determinant of homeownership status.

The amount of accommodation bond that a resident will be asked to pay will be determined by a number of factors including: the location of the facility, age of the facility, debt from construction or refurbishment, house prices in the area, the standard of other facilities in the area, the price of accommodation bonds at other facilities, demand for the service, the anticipated level of funding that will be received for the resident and the resident's capacity to pay.

Facilities will generally have one of two approaches: Assets Assessment or Market Price.

Assets Assessment—the facility will ask the resident to complete the Asset Assessment booklet and, once the assessable assets have been determined by the government, will then either negotiate an amount of accommodation bond up to the amount stated in the asset assessment, charge the maximum amount as stated in the asset assessment letter or choose not to accept the resident.

Market Price—the facility will tell you what the accommodation bond is for a given room or for the facility as a whole (depending on whether their market price is based on different rooms with different sizes, views, proximity to gardens/nurses stations/common areas etc or just a "one price for all" model). Often this amount serves as a base from which residents or their adviser can negotiate a higher amount in exchange for a discount or agree some other financial arrangement to meet the ongoing cost of care.

Aged Care Facilities cannot charge a resident an accommodation bond that is greater than their assessable assets minus the minimum assets amount. Remember, however, that an aged care facility doesn't have to accept a resident or any given financial arrangement. The Residential Care Agreement (RCA) entered into by the facility and the resident must be by mutual agreement. This should always be kept in mind when considering appropriate strategies for meeting aged care costs, as accessing aged care under certain financial arrangements may be difficult or impossible. An example of this would be a Supported Resident who wanted to access an extra services bed. With no requirement to maintain a ratio of Supported Residents and no

Supported Resident funding from the government, it is highly unlikely the facility would accept this and the resident would need to accept a standard care bed.

Family members often think that they can "pass the hat around" and pay the bond on behalf of the resident. Provided that the resident has not yet been admitted as a Supported Resident and/or has not provided a copy of the asset assessment letter showing they have insufficient assets to pay the bond, this may be possible.

> **Note: Family members who loan money to the resident to pay either the accommodation bond or ongoing fees and charges (or both) should seek legal advice about documenting the transactions. An accommodation bond paid to an aged care facility is refunded to the estate of the resident and distributed in accordance with their will, irrespective of who paid it.**

Retention amount

Retention amount is a fee that is normally deducted from the accommodation bond (lump sum) on a monthly basis for a maximum of five years. In some cases the retention amount is charged to the resident on a daily/monthly basis.

The maximum amount of retention a resident can pay is set by the government at the date of entry and does not vary. There are two levels of retention, based on the amount of accommodation bond the resident has paid and the date of entry. For people who pay a bond amount greater than $38,160—the majority of bond payers—the retention is currently $318p.m. capped at $19,080 after five years. For people who pay a bond of $19,740 or less the retention amount is $164.50p.m. capped at $9,870 after five years. And for those whose bond amount falls in between, the retention is 10% of the bond amount divided by 12. For example, if you paid a bond of $25,000 on 1 June 2011 your retention amount would be $2,500÷12=$208.33p.m. capped at $12,500 after five years. If a resident lives in care for two months, or less, retention can be charged for the month that the resident moved in plus the following two months. The retention amount is not affected by the amount paid; rather it is determined by the total bond amount.

Retention amounts

For residents entering care in the period For	For bonds of at least	Maximum monthly retention
1 Jul 2011–30 Jun 2012	$38,160	$318.00
1 Jul 2010–30 Jun 2011	$36,900	$307.50
1 Jul 2009–30 Jun 2010	$35,880	$299.00
1 Jul 2008–30 Jun 2009	$35,040	$292.00
1 Jul 2007–30 Jun 2008	$33,600	$280.00
1 Jul 2006–30 Jun 2007	$32,820	$273.50
1 Jul 2005–30 Jun 2006	$31,860	$265.50
For bonds up to the lower threshold		
1 Jul 2011–30 Jun 2012	$19,740	$164.50
1 Jul 2010–30 Jun 2011	$19,080	$159.00
1 Jul 2009–30 Jun 2010	$18,540	$154.50
1 Jul 2008–30 Jun 2009	$18,120	$151.00

1 Jul 2007–30 Jun 2008	$17,400	$145.00
1 Jul 2006–30 Jun 2007	$16,980	$141.50
1 Jul 2005–30 Jun 2006	$16,500	$137.50

Periodic interest payment

The amount of interest charged on any amount of unpaid bond is capped at the Maximum Permissible Interest Rate (MPIR) that applies at the date of permanent entry. The amount of interest charged on any amount of unpaid bond can be negotiated between the facility and the resident but cannot exceed the MPIR that applies at the date of permanent entry. The interest rate is set by the Department of Health and Ageing at three percentage points lower than the Australian Tax Office General Interest Charge.

The maximum permissible interest rate payable is:

Residents who entered care between	Maximum Permissible Interest Rate
1 Jul 2011–30 Sep 2011	9.00%
1 Apr 2011–30 Jun 2011	8.92%
1 Jan 2011–31 Mar 2011	9.02%
1 Oct 2010–31 Dec 2010	8.74%
1 Jul 2010–30 Sep 2010	8.80%

1 Apr 2010–30 Jun 2010	8.16%
1 Jan 2010–31 Mar 2010	7.95%
1 Oct 2009–31 Dec 2009	7.30%
1 Jul 2009–30 Sep 2009	7.13%
1 Apr 2009–30 Jun 2009	7.16%
1 Jan 2009–31 Mar 2009	8.76%
1 Oct 2008–31 Dec 2008	11.31%
1 Jul 2008–30 Sep 2008	11.75%
1 Apr 2008–30 Jun 2008	11.69%
1 Jan 2008–31 Mar 2008	11.15%
1 Oct 2007–31 Dec 2007	10.75%
1 Jan 2007–30 Sep 2007	10.37%
1 Oct 2006–31 Dec 2006	10.19%
1 Jul 2006–30 Sep 2006	9.87%
1 Apr 2006–30 Jun 2006	9.61%
1 Jan 2006–31 Mar 2006	9.63%
1 Oct 2005–31 Dec 2005	9.62%
1 Jul 2005–30 Sep 2005	9.68%

Where none of the bond is paid by lump sum (or only a small amount) the periodic payment will be calculated as the interest on the outstanding amount plus retention, and will generally be charged on a monthly basis.

Refunding the bond

The balance of the accommodation bond will generally be refunded to you or your estate soon after you leave the facility.

Reason	When the bond must be refunded
You leave the facility and return home	Within 14 days after you leave
You pass away	Within 14 days of confirmation of probate or a letter of administration being received.
You move to another facility and provide at least 14 days notice	On the day that you move
You move to another facility and provide less than 14 days notice	Within 14 days of when you provided the notice
You move to another facility with no notice being provided	Within 14 days of the day you move
The facility ceases to be certified	Within 14 days of the date certification ceases

Since 1 July 2006 aged care facilities have been required to pay interest on a resident's bond for the period of time after the resident leaves the facility until the accommodation bond balance is refunded to them/their estate.

Two rates of interest apply based on when the bond is refunded: the Base Interest Rate and the Maximum Permissible Interest Rate.

Base Interest Rate and the Maximum Permissible Interest Rate. **Base Interest**

Rate is charged from the day after the resident moves out until the end of the legislated timeframe. For example, a resident who moves to another facility with no notice being provided will have the base rate of interest applied to their bond for the period of time after they leave until the expiry of the 14 day period. The interest is calculated on a daily basis—if the facility refunds the bond within 10 days then interest is only payable for those 10 days.

If the facility does not refund the bond within the legislated timeframe interest will be charged at the **Maximum Permissible Interest Rate** from the end of the legislated timeframe until the bond is refunded.

> *Note regarding changes in interest rates: The amount of Base Interest Rate or Maximum Permissible Interest Rate that applies to the bond is determined by the date after the resident leaves and the date after the legislated timeframe expired. The interest rate is fixed at those dates and is not affected by any future rate changes.*

If the resident leaves	Base Interest Rate (p.a.)	Max. Permissible Interest Rate (p.a.)
1 Jul 2011–30 Sep 2011	5%	9.00%
1 Apr 2011–30 Jun 2011	5%	8.92%
1 Jan 2011–30 Mar 2011	5%	9.02%
1 Oct 2010–31 Dec 2010	5%	8.74%
1 Jul 2010–30 Sep 2010	5%	8.80%
1 Apr 2010–30 Jun 2010	5%	8.16%
1 Jan 2010–31 Mar 2010	4%	7.95%
1 Oct 2009–31 Dec 2009	4%	7.30%
1 Jul 2009–30 Sep 2009	4%	7.13%
1 Apr 2009–30 Jun 2009	4%	7.16%
1 Jan 2009–31 Mar 2009	5%	8.76%
17 Nov 2008–31 Dec 2008	5%	11.31%
1 Oct 2008–16 Nov 2008	6%	11.31%

Protection of the accommodation bond

On 31 May 2006 the government guaranteed the accommodation bond paid to an approved provider. A number of requirements relating to accommodation bonds were also placed on aged care facilities at this time.

From 1 July 2006 approved providers are required to meet new prudential requirements:

Liquidity Standard—ensure that there are sufficient liquid funds available to meet the anticipated accommodation bond refund obligations for the next 12 months through a Liquidity Management Strategy

Records Standard—provide accurate, comprehensive and up-to-date information on bond holdings through a Bond Register and maintain these records for a minimum of three years

Disclosure Standard—all providers holding accommodation bonds (including pre-1997 Entry Contributions) must provide the Department of Health and Ageing, residents (and their representatives) and prospective residents information about their compliance and bond holdings annually and provide residents who pay a bond a copy of the accommodation bond agreement and bond guarantee.

Approved providers are required to adhere to these requirements, are provided with education and materials to assist them and are subject to ongoing monitoring of compliance. However, the government does not regulate their investment decisions and there are no restrictions on the way in which the monies are invested.

If an approved provider becomes insolvent or bankrupt and defaults on its obligation to refund accommodation bonds, the Australian Government Accommodation Bond Guarantee Scheme under the *Aged Care (Bond Security) Act 2006* provides a guarantee to refund the accommodation bond balance to the resident or their estate.

While it has never yet been put into practice, the Act enables the government to recover costs that cannot be recovered from the provider via a levy on other approved providers holding accommodation bonds.

Chapter 17

Daily care fees & income tested fees

Basic daily care fee

The daily care fee for residents who entered an aged care facility prior to 20 March 2008 was based on whether or not they were receiving an income support payment, the amount of accommodation bond they paid and whether or not they disclosed their financial information to Centrelink at the time of entry. People in receipt of an income support payment (even $1) who had not paid an accommodation bond above the threshold at the time were classified as pensioners and paid the (lower) pensioner rate of daily care fee. People who had paid an accommodation bond above the threshold or who had not disclosed their financial information to Centrelink were classified as "non-pensioners" and paid the "non-pensioner" rate of daily care fee.

Why is this important? Because the amount of daily care fee you can be asked to pay will depend on your classification when you entered. For residents who entered care on or after 20 March 2008 the Basic Daily Care was calculated at 85% of the full basic pension for all residents.

On 20 September 2009, however, changes were made to aged care fees and charges to reflect the significant changes made to pension payments in the 2009 Budget.

To ensure that aged care providers were able to meet increasing costs while residents were left with sufficient to cover incidental expenses, the daily care fee for full pensioners and part pensioners with low levels of private income was set at 84% of the new basic pension.

Protection measures were introduced for part pensioners and self funded retirees who would not receive an increase in pension equal to the increase in daily care fee and were already living in care, and a phasing in of the new daily care fee was introduced for part pensioners and self funded retirees who enter care after 20 September.

The following table shows the private income thresholds that have been applicable since these changes were introduced:

Effective date	Single	Couple (each)
1 July 2011	$387.50	$369.50
20 March 2011	$383.50	$365.50
20 September 2010	$379.10	$361.10
1 July 2010	$374.10	$356.10
20 March 2010	$370.10	$352.10
20 September 2009	$360.00	$342.00

Four categories of resident classification were introduced, standard, phased, non-standard and protected, with the following definitions applying:

Standard resident—a resident who is a full pensioner or part pensioner with private income below the threshold. This classification applies to the majority of aged care residents.

Protected resident—a resident who was in permanent care prior to 20 September 2009 and is a part pensioner or self funded retiree with private income above $360 pfn (single) or $342 pfn (couple each). Protected residents had their daily care fee "protected" and any increase to their daily care fee is in line with the Consumer Price Index (CPI).

Phased resident—a part pensioner or self funded retiree with private income above the threshold who entered care after 20 September 2009. The daily care fee as a percentage of the pension increases by 1% every 20 March and September until 20 March 2013 when it equals the Standard Residents' fee.

77 per cent between 20 September 2009 and 19 March 2010
78 per cent between 20 March 2010 and 19 September 2010
79 per cent between 20 September 2010 and 19 March 2011
80 per cent between 20 March 2011 and 19 September 2011
81 per cent between 20 September 2011 and 19 March 2012
82 per cent between 20 March 2012 and 19 September 2012
83 per cent between 20 September 2012 and 19 March 2013

84 per cent from 20 March 2013

Non-standard resident (formerly non-pensioner)—a resident who entered care prior to 20 March 2008 and did not disclose their financial information or agreed to pay a bond greater than the limit at that time or was a self funded retiree.

While the resident classification is based on your level of private income at the date of permanent entry, changes to your income can change your status. For example, a resident who moved into aged care last week as a part pensioner with private income in excess of the threshold may sell some investments to pay the accommodation bond. If this resulted in a reduction of private income below the threshold the resident's classification would change from Phased to Standard.

Income tested fee

The daily income tested fee is calculated after a resident moves in and is based on their—and (if applicable) their partner's—assessable income.

Prior to 20 March 2008 the income tested fee threshold was based on the allowable income to receive the full pension ($3,432p.a. single and $6,032p.a. couple) with means tested pensions being exempt. This meant that pensioners could earn the full pension plus the allowed income while self funded retirees could only earn the allowed income before paying an income tested fee.

Assessable income earned in excess of the threshold attracted an income tested fee at 25¢ per dollar, capped based on whether or not the resident was a pensioner. From 20 March 2008 the income tested fee threshold was lifted, with the new threshold equal to the full pension plus the allowable income to receive the full pension. Income earned in excess of the threshold attracted an Income Tested Fee at 41.67¢ per dollar, capped based on whether or not the resident was a pensioner.

The income tested fee is like a co-contribution between the resident and the government up to the cost of care. It is important to realise that an aged care facility does not receive any more money from a resident who pays an income tested fee than from one who doesn't. The income tested fee simply reduces the level of funding that the facility receives from the government on a dollar for dollar basis. For example, if a facility was eligible for $55 per day government funding for a resident and the resident was liable to pay an income tested fee of $20 per day, the amount of government contribution would reduce to $35.

Since 20 September 2009 the income tested fee threshold is now set according to the resident's classification. Income tested fees are calculated at 41.67¢ per dollar of income in excess of the threshold.

Income tested fee thresholds as at 1 July 2011

Resident classification	Income tested fee threshold (pfn) Single	Income tested fee threshold (pfn) Couple (each)
Standard and non-standard	$847.90	$829.90
Protected	$754.30	$736.30
Phased	$794.45	$776.45

Income tested fees are capped at $64.69 per day. People who do not disclose their income, a single person with around $78,000p.a. of assessable income or a couple with around $154,000p.a. of assessable income or more will pay the maximum income tested fee.

Income tested fees are not charged where the calculated amount is less than $1 per day.

> **People who cannot be charged an income tested fee:**
> - Full pensioners
> - Residents in respite
> - Ex prisoners of war
> - Residents with a dependent child
> - Residents who entered care between 1 October 1997 and 28 February 1998.

> *The income tested fee is re-calculated quarterly: January, March, July and September, and you and the facility are advised in writing each time. If your income or cost of care changes during the period a refund can be issued. However, if your assessable income increases you will not be charged extra for that period.*

The formula for calculating the income tested fee is simply:

Total assessable income less income tested fee threshold x 41.67¢

It is important to be aware the your sources of income will be assessed according to social security rules rather than actual or taxable income.

Deeming

Irrespective of whether or not you are a pensioner, your income tested fee is calculated by Centrelink or DVA in accordance with their income tests. The way in which income will be assessed on your bank accounts, shares, managed funds and other financial assets including loans, gold and other bullion and friendly society or life insurance bonds is by applying deeming rates. Deeming is also applied to any gifts (in excess of $10,000 in a financial year or $30,000 in a five-year period) made within five years of entering aged care or while living in aged care.

Deeming is a relatively simple way of determining income, with one rate applied to the lower amount of assets and another rate applied to assets above this amount. To calculate the deemed income you simply add the two figures together.

Current deeming rates (as at 1 July 2011) are:

Single	Deeming rates
First $44,600	3%
Assets above	4.5%
Couple	
First $74,400	3%
Assets above	4.5%

For example, a single person with $135,000 of financial assets would be deemed to earn:
$5,406 p.a. ($44,600x3%=$1,338+$90,400x4.5%=$4,068)

While a couple with the same amount of financial assets would be deemed to earn:
$4,959 p.a. ($74,400x3%=$2,232+$60,600x4.5%=$2,727)

Actual income

Income streams such as annuities, defined benefit income streams and superannuation pensions are generally assessed based on the amount received less adjustment for a deductible component.

Defined benefit superannuation

Usually only people who have worked in the public sector or in large companies will have a Defined Benefit Superannuation fund. They differ from an accumulation fund where the balance of the account is always visible and will fluctuate in line with the assets held by the fund as the benefits are usually based on a formula, for example, 5.4 x final salary. This formula usually takes into account the age at which you retired, your period of service and your last year's salary, or some other salary benchmark.

Because defined benefit super income streams don't normally have an identifiable account balance they are not subject to an assets test. They are subject to the income test, less allowance for the deductible component, but in most cases it is impossible to determine what this is without contacting the fund and Centrelink or Department of Veterans' Affairs.

Asset test exempt income streams

This is a long term income stream that was purchased before 20 September 2007, and which is payable for the lifetime of the beneficiary, or where the term is based on the life expectancy of the beneficiary(ies).

Asset Test exempt income streams are required to:
- Make an income payment at least annually

- Have a Nil Residual Capital Value.
  Furthermore:
- the entire purchase price must have been converted to income payments
- the payments must have been fixed at the start and indexed at a maximum of 5% or CPI+1%
- the payments cannot decrease (except after an allowed commutation)
- the investment can only be commuted in limited circumstances
- the investment cannot be used as security for borrowing.

The assessable income of asset test exempt income streams is calculated as:

$$\text{Annual Payment} - \left(\frac{\text{Purchase Price}}{\text{Relevant Number}}\right)$$

For income streams purchased prior to 20 September 2004 a 100% asset test exemption will apply. Income streams purchased on or after 20 September 2004 and prior to 20 September 2007 have a 50% asset test exemption. Income streams purchased after 20 September 2007 or that don't meet the criteria are 100% assessable.

Although unlikely, if a commutation is used to purchase the income stream the purchase price will need to be adjusted as per the long-term income stream calculation below.

> *For example:*
> *A complying annuity purchased for $200,000 with a term of 10 years would have a deductible amount of $20,000. If the annual payment was $27,500 the assessable income for income test purposes would be $7,500.*

We appreciate that these calculations are complex which is why we strongly suggest that you consult with your advisor to ensure the calculations are done properly and the outcome is in your best interests.

Long-term income streams

Long-term income streams generally have a term of more than five years or are equal to or greater than life expectancy on commencement. They include lifetime annuities, term allocated pensions and account based pensions and they are treated the same way in determining income irrespective of whether they were purchased with superannuation money or private money.

The assessable income of a long-term income stream is calculated as:

$$\text{Annual Payment} - \left(\frac{\text{Purchase Price} - \text{Commutation Amounts} - \text{Residual Capital}}{\text{Relevant Number}} \right)$$

For example, a lifetime annuity (indexed at CPI) purchased today for $250,000 would provide an income in the first year of $20,351.81, with future annual income being this amount (indexed at CPI) for the life of that person. Assuming there are no commutations, the deductible amount would be $30,560 each year, meaning that none of the payment would be assessable until it exceeds $30,560p.a.

Short-term income streams

Short-term income streams generally have a term of five years or less and can have a residual capital value of anywhere between 0–100%. These income streams are fully assessable for determining assessable assets and, unlike their long-term counterparts, income is determined using the deeming method.

This means that the entire account balance is subject to deeming for the income test. Where the residual capital value is 100% the account balance will remain unchanged for the life of the income stream. However, where the residual capital value is less than 100% deeming will be applied to the new (reduced) account balance each year.

For example, an annuity purchased for $100,000 at 5% interest with a term of four years and an RCV 100 would provide $5,000 income each year with the capital being refunded at the end of the four years. However, the assessment of the income wouldn't be the $5,000 but would be based on the deemed income on $100,000. Assuming there are other financial assets of more than $44,600, the deemed income on the annuity would $4,500 per year.

Investment properties/trusts/companies

Investment properties, trusts and company structures are assessed based on the actual (taxable) income earned. Trust and company structures have their ownership determined based on attribution tests of source and control.

Source Test: where did the money or the asset come from

Control Test: who controls, or could reasonably expect to control, the entity.

Based on the outcome of these two tests, the asset and income will be attributed to someone or a group of people in percentage terms.

It is important to be aware that the tax treatment of the assets and income is completely different to the Centrelink/DVA Assessment. For example, Mum and Dad are the only contributors to their trust and are also Trustees and Appointers. The Centrelink/DVA attribution tests will attribute 100% of the assets and income to Mum and Dad even if they distribute income to their children or other beneficiaries of the trust for tax purposes.

War widows and other compensation payment recipients

Even though compensation payments such as the War Widows Pension and other foreign periodic compensation payments are exempt from the calculation of income for other purposes such as the calculation of means tested pensions and the calculation of tax, these payments are considered to be income for the purpose of calculating the income tested fee.

For war widows who also receive the Income Support Supplement this often means that they will exceed the income tested fee threshold. The War Widows Pension is a non means tested amount of $738.70pfn and the Income Support Supplement, which is means tested, is $220.80 at full rate. A war widow receiving these payments would be considered to be a phased resident (as her private income exceeds the threshold) and thus her income tested fee threshold is $794.45pfn while her DVA payments total $959.50pfn. This means her income tested fee (with no other income) would be around $5 per day. Such an outcome often comes as a shock to war widows and other compensation payment recipients as it is inconsistent with the way in which their income is normally treated.

SECTION 4

Financial strategies for residential aged care

The eight chapters in this section cover some of the key financial strategies that could enable you to make a move into residential aged care more affordable both at the time of moving and on an ongoing basis.

Most often the person moving into aged care is a single person whose partner is no longer alive and who has been living alone in their own home. The complexities of the decisions now facing them can seem overwhelming but these more than double when dealing with a couple.

Unfortunately, many people focus on the accommodation bond and meeting the cost of care on day one, with little or no thought to the funding of care in the longer term. When it is one member of a couple moving into care, the tendency to focus on the cost of care and ways to meet this expense often overlooks the cost of living for the person remaining in the family home. The cost of living for the person who remains in the family home does not halve when the other member of the couple lives in aged care. Insurance, rates, electricity, water etc are unlikely to change very much. But the collective costs of living can increase significantly.

Timing can be critical. And we are not just talking about the personal decision of when you feel ready for residential aged care. The timing of your assets assessment plays a very important part.

Many people assume they will have to sell the family home to go into residential care. That isn't the best course of action for everyone—as we'll explain.

We also look at how paying more than you are being asked to for an accommodation bond could leave you with *more* money in your pocket!

Of course, not all of the strategies will fit all of the people reading this book. You, your family and your advisers must ultimately decide what is best for your care needs and financial situation. What we are aiming to do is enable you to understand your options.

Chapter 18

Keeping the former home

Too often people assume that they will be forced to sell their home to fund the move to aged care. Of course, for some, selling up will be the right decision but it is important to be aware that there are special rules that apply to the former home when you move to aged care.

For two years from the date you or your partner move out, the former home is exempt from the assets used in calculating your pension entitlement. The purpose of this rule is to enable you to move back to the home if you are able to do so.

The other set of rules that can apply enable you to keep and rent your former home with a number of exemptions applying to the asset and the income (rent). To do this the resident must meet the following criteria:

- pay at least part of an accommodation bond by periodic payment OR
- pay an accommodation charge
- AND rent out the former home.

Note that fully supported residents do not meet the criteria as they are not able to pay an accommodation bond or accommodation charge.

Where these criteria are met the former home and any rent received is exempt from the following:
- the calculation of pension entitlement under the asset test
- the calculation of pension entitlement under the income test
- the calculation of the daily income tested fee.

> ***Important: don't confuse these asset exemptions with those used to determine assessable assets for calculating the maximum amount of accommodation bond or accommodation charge.***

While the rent you charge doesn't have to be at market rates, you do need to show some genuine rent income for the exemptions to apply. If the criteria are not met then the two-year general exemption will apply.

Points to consider

There are other factors you need to take into account before your make your decision:

Capital requirement—you may have to spend money to bring the house up to a standard suitable for a rental

Ongoing maintenance—you'll need to have capital and/or available income to cover ongoing maintenance and repairs

Costs—whether you rent it out commercially or for nominal rent to a child/grandchild, there are expenses associated with keeping the property such as rates and insurance and, perhaps, agents' fees and income tax

Capital gains tax—if the house is rented for more than six years there may be CGT consequences on the sale of the house which also need to be factored in

Insurance—while it may be a financially viable option to keep the former home vacant, with the two-year exemption applying, you should be aware that the home and contents insurance is likely to lapse 30–60 days after the home has been vacated. Similarly, if you choose to keep and rent the house you should discuss with your insurer a change of policy to landlord's insurance which may provide you with extra protection against damage caused by tenants or tenants defaulting on rent.

What about tax?

The rent you receive is exempt from the calculation of pension entitlement and daily income tested fees (where the above criteria are met) but don't forget that it will be assessable as income for tax purposes and will need to be declared. This does not necessarily mean that you will have to pay tax. However, you must also bear in mind that if you are accepting less than market rent, full tax deductions may not be applicable to the costs associated with renting the home.

Which is best?

So, sell the former home to fund the accommodation bond and hang on to any income-producing assets such as shares or term deposits etc? Or rent the home out to produce income and use the cash assets for the bond? Because of the asset and income exemptions that can apply, as well as the tax advantaged position of many residents, using assets that would normally be assessable and deemed to earn income to pay a portion of the accommodation bond while renting the former home may deliver a more beneficial outcome. It is likely to produce an increase in pension and a lower daily income tested fee than the other option.

Of course, you also need to take into account the different financial arrangements that apply to different types of care. The following examines two of the possible scenarios in deciding to move into aged care—paying an accommodation bond or paying accommodation charges—while keeping and renting out the former home.

Case Study

Tom is a part age pensioner (currently receiving $551.93pfn/$14,350.05p.a.) and has recently been assessed as requiringhigh care. He has found an aged care facility that he likes close to where he currently lives and one of his children. Tom has stated that his main financial objective is to retain his home and the family has received an estimated market rent from a local real estate agent of $350p.w.

The facility has offered the choice of an extra services bed with an

accommodation bond of $300,000 and a daily extra service fee of $15p.d., or a standard bed with an accommodation charge of $30.55p.d.

Tom's assets are:

House	$700,000
Cash	$50,000
Term deposits	$100,000
Shares	$150,000
Contents/personal effects	$5,000

Standard bed cost of care:

Daily care fee (phased)	$38.33 p.d.
Accommodation charge	$30.55 p.d.
Income tested fee	$6.52 p.d.
Total cost of care	$27,521.00
+ *chocolates, haircuts & outings*	$2,600
	= $30,121.00

Income:

Pension	$14,350.05
Interest/dividends	$15,000
Rent	$18,200
	= $47,550.05 p.a.

Whether Tom rents his home for $1p.w. or market rent the above figures would remain unchanged in terms of the cost of care and pension entitlement. His cash flow position is almost neutral so this would obviously alter based on the amount of rent received.

Extra Services

If Tom uses $285,000 of his deemed assets to pay towards his accommodation bond, paying the remaining $15,000 by periodic payment, his financial situation will be:

House	$700,000
Cash	$15,000
Contents/personal effects	$5,000

Cost of care:

Daily care fee	$40.25 p.d.
Periodic payment	$3.70 p.d.
Extra service fee	$15 p.d.
Income tested fee	$0 p.d.
Total cost of care	$21,516.75
+ *chocolates, haircuts & outings*	$2,600
	= $24,116.75

Income:

Pension entitlement	$18,961.80	p.a.
Interest	$750	p.a.
Rent	$18,200	p.a. *($350p.w.)*
	= $37,911.80	

As you can see, if Tom didn't receive the rent for his home in this situation he would have a negative cash flow position of $4,404.95p.a. Due to the low level of liquid assets he now has, he would exhaust his funds in around 3.5 years or would need to consider a reverse mortgage.

Holiday homes and investment properties

Your holiday home or investment property is an assessable asset for both pension and aged care purposes. However, it is important to understand that these assets, including vacant blocks of land, are not *deemed* to earn income—only actual income or taxable income received is used to calculate pension entitlement (under the income test) as well as your resident classification and the daily income tested fee.

The exemptions that can be applied to the asset and the income derived from the former home that we looked at earlier cannot be applied here. In considering whether to retain or sell a holiday home or an investment property to fund aged care, there are a number of key considerations:

- The value of each property in relation to the amount of money required
- The amount of income (rent) the investment property or holiday home does or could produce
- Cost of selling
- Cost of keeping
- What will be done with any excess funds—any proceeds from the sale placed in bank accounts, term deposits, shares (deemed

assets) will be deemed to earn income for pension and income tested fee purposes
- Any CGT consequences of the sale need to be considered. Unlike shares, which can be sold in instalments or in the exact amount needed, the home will be realised as a lump sum in a single financial year and, as such, you will need to consider the impact of any other CGT events in that year as well as any losses or offsets that can be put against the tax liability. It is also important to consider what the likely impact of the sale would be in the event of property being sold after the death of the owner. In many cases the best tax outcome will be if the house is sold while the owner is alive, with the tax offsets that apply to the cost of care being used to minimise the liability.
- The pension consequences
- The impact on the cost of care.

Case Study

Fred is currently a part pensioner (receiving $241.43pfn/$6,277.18p.a.) living in his own home. He has recently been assessed as requiring low care and has found a facility nearby that has quoted him a bond of $350,000.

Fred's assets are:

House	$650,000 *(estimated net rent $400p.w.)*
Investment property	$450,000 *(net rent $350p.w.)*
Cash	$60,000
Personal effects	$2,000

Let's look at what would happen if Fred sells his investment property to fund his accommodation bond or sells his home.

Selling the investment property

If Fred sells his investment property to fund his accommodation bond, leaving $10,000 of the bond outstanding to enable him to meet the asset and income exemptions, his cost of care would be:

Accommodation bond	$340,000
Daily care fee	$40.25 p.d.
Periodic payment	$2.47 p.d.
Income tested fee	$1.76 p.d.
Total	$16,235.20
+ *chocolates, haircuts & outings*	$2,600
	= $18,835.20 p.a.

Income:

Pension	$17,421.30 p.a.	*($670.05 pfn)*
Interest	$8,500 p.a.	
Rent	$20,800 p.a.	
	= $46,721.30 p.a.	

Selling the home & renting the investment property

If Fred sold his home instead and rented his investment property, he cannot meet the criteria for an asset and income test exemption, so his cost of care would be:

Accommodation bond	$350,000
Daily care fee	$38.33 p.d.
Periodic payment	$0 p.d.
Income tested fee	$14.97 p.d.
Total	$19,545.50
+ *chocolates, haircuts & outings*	$2,600
=	$22,054.50 p.a.

Income:

Pension	$0	p.a.
Interest	$18,000	p.a.
Rent	$18,200	p.a.
=	$36,200	p.a.

When you compare the two scenarios you can see that the assessable income from the investment property combined with an increase in deemed income has a significant impact on Fred's pension entitlement (a reduction of $17,421.30p.a.) and income tested fee (an increase of $4,821.65p.a.).

> ***Fred could utilise other strategies to improve his pension and cost of aged care positions, such as paying a bigger accommodation bond in exchange for a discount on his aged care fees or using a trust structure.***

Chapter 19

Reverse Mortgages

A reverse mortgage enables you to withdraw equity from your home as a lump sum, regular payment or a combination of the two. The amount you can borrow through a reverse mortgage will depend on the value of your house and the age of the youngest borrower. Generally speaking, the older you are the more you can borrow.

Unlike a normal mortgage, where you need both the asset to back the loan and the income to service it, a reverse mortgage doesn't require you to make repayments. While this may seem attractive, it is important to be aware of the capitalisation of interest and the effect this has on your debt position. Compound interest is a great tool for saving but it's a heavy burden for debt. Reverse mortgage interest rates also tend to be higher than general mortgage rates as the level of risk to the lender is higher.

The use of reverse mortgages to meet an accommodation bond is a common strategy and often directly related to the desire to keep and rent the former home. Reverse mortgages can be a necessity when there is insufficient capital outside the house to pay towards the accommodation bond to minimise the periodic payment and/or there is insufficient income to meet the periodic payment.

If the long term objective is to retain the home, serious consideration needs to be given to how this debt will be met when the elderly person passes away. In particular, it will be important to understand the compound interest nature of the loan, any costs associated with establishing the facility, any penalties associated with discharging the debt (this is likely if the interest rate is fixed), the potential impact if interest rates change, as well as any assumed growth rate on the property and how changes in this will affect the ability to repay or transfer the debt at a later time. You need to weigh up very seriously the outcome of paying the accommodation bond by periodic payment—if the aged care facility will allow—against the use of a reverse mortgage.

> *Note—the payment of interest on a reverse mortgage does not meet the exemption criteria for keeping and renting the former home. If the objective is to utilise these rules the accommodation bond should still be paid part by lump sum with the remainder via periodic payment. If the bond is paid in full, the two-year general exemption will apply to the asset, with any income being assessed based on the net rent received.*

Case Study

Lizzie is 85, currently receives the full age pension ($729.30pfn) and has been assessed as requiring low care. The accommodation bond at the facility she likes is $300,000. The family has received advice and quotes and believes it will require $20,000 to bring the house up to a rentable standard.

Lizzie's assets are:

House	$650,000
Cash	$50,000 *(less $20,000 for renovations)*
Contents/personal effects	$2,000
Rent	$350 p.w.

With no reverse mortgage her financial situation would be:

Cost of care:

Daily care fee	$40.25 p.d.
Periodic payment	$73.97 p.d.
Income tested fee	$0
Retention fee	$10.45 p.d.
Total	$45,504.55 p.a.
+ *chocolates, haircuts & outings*	$2,600 p.a.
=	$48,104.55 p.a.

Income:

Pension entitlement	$18,961.80 p.a. *($729.30pfn)*
Interest	$1,500.00 p.a.
Rent	$18,200 p.a. *($350p.w.)*
Total	$38,661.80 p.a.
Cash flow deficit	$9,442.75 p.a.

Lizzie would run out of capital in around 4.5 years. If she didn't renovate her home, thereby retaining her $50,000 in cash, and rented it to her grandson for $1p.w. plus outgoings (rates and insurance), her cash flow deficit would be $26,642.75 per year and would exhaust her capital in less than 2 years.

> *Of course, Lizzie could decide at that time to use a reverse mortgage to pay a lump sum towards her accommodation bond*

> *or as a line of credit to meet her cash flow deficit.*

Using a reverse mortgage

If Lizzie used a reverse mortgage at 8% to fund $290,000 of her accommodation bond, paying $10,000 by periodic payment to the aged care facility, her situation would be:

Cost of care:

Daily care fee	$40.25	p.d.
Periodic payment	$2.47	p.d.
Income tested fee	$0	
(Retention of $307.50 would be deducted from the bond paid)		
Total	$15,592.80	p.a.
+ *chocolates, haircuts & outings*	$2,600	p.a.
=	$18,192.80	p.a.

Income:

Pension entitlement	$18,961.80	p.a. *($729.30pfn)*
Interest	$1,500	p.a.
Rent	$18,200	p.a. *($350p.w.)*
Total	$38,661.80	p.a.
Cash flow	$20,469	p.a.

If Lizzie used the rent received to make repayments of $1,500 per month to the reverse mortgage her debt position would be $321,000 after 5 years.

> *If she decided to rent her home to her grandson for $1 p.w. plus outgoings, her cash flow would be neutral and the interest on her reverse mortgage would capitalise. Her debt position after five years would be $443,000.*

Case Study

Let's look at another example:

Jeff and Dot have lived in their own home for 60 years and for the last four years Dot has cared for Jeff with a little support from home care. However, Jeff's health has now deteriorated to the point that he needs more care than Dot and home care can provide. He has been assessed by the **ACAT** as requiring Low Care.

Their current assets are:

Home	$500,000
Bank accounts	$50,000
Term deposits	$320,000
Car	$20,000
Contents	$15,000

Jeff and Dot both currently live very comfortably on a part pension and the income from their bank accounts and term deposits.

The aged care facility Dot would like Jeff to move to has quoted an accommodation bond of $300,000 and explained that they set their bonds on a market price basis, with a number of beds reserved for fully supported residents (those with less than $39,000). They have advised that any amount of the bond that is unpaid will have interest payable at 9.00% and this could be deducted from the bond paid.

If Jeff and Dot were to submit to an asset assessment the maximum amount of accommodation bond Jeff could be asked to pay is $163,500. However, as the facility won't accept this, Dot either needs to find one that would, or fund the bond of $300,000. Obviously Dot's concern is that the payment of the bond will significantly reduce the income they receive. Will she have enough to cover her costs in remaining at home and for the care Jeff needs? She has also been told that as a part pensioner Jeff may need to pay an income tested fee, which will be calculated after he enters care.

Dot estimates her cost of living at $25,000 and believes Jeff will need $50p.w. in addition to his cost of care for chocolates, haircuts and outings.

Dot is unsure of the best way to fund the bond and the implications this may

> *have on their pension entitlement and Jeff's cost of care.*

When Jeff moves to aged care, their pension will change to be that of an illness separated couple. Here's how the situation would look if Jeff and Dot pay $250,000 of the accommodation bond by lump sum, with interest charged on the $50,000 outstanding deducted from this amount:

Lump sum payment of accommodation bond—in part—from current assets

Cost of care:

Daily care fee	$40.25	p.d.
Periodical payment on unpaid bond *(deducted from the bond)*	$12.33	p.d.
Income tested fee	$0	
Total	$14,691.25	p.a.
+ *chocolates, haircuts & outings*	$2,600	p.a.
=	$17,291.25	

Income:

Pension	$37,923.60	p.a. *($729.30 each pfn)*
Interest	$6,000	
Total	$43,923.60	

Their cash flow can meet the cost of care; however, if the bond was funded in full or the interest payable monthly they would have insufficient cash flow to meet the combined cost of living. Of course the periodical payment, along with retention, is reducing the amount of the bond paid back at the end by around $8,300p.a. for the first five years, then $4,500p.a. after that.

Many people in this situation will assume that a reverse mortgage to fund the bond would be a better option, as the liquid funds are then preserved and able to produce the necessary income. Let's look at what would happen if $250,000 were taken as a reverse mortgage with interest on the unpaid bond paid daily.

Reverse mortgage to fund bond

Home	$500,000
(less reverse mortgage $250,000)	
Bank accounts	$50,000
Term deposits	$320,000
Car	$20,000
Contents	$15,000

Cost of care:

Daily care fee	$40.25 p.d.
Periodical payment	$12.33 p.d.
Income tested fee	$1.84 p.d.
Total	$19,863.30
+ *chocolates, haircuts & outings*	$2,600 p.a.
=	$22,463.30

Income:

Pension entitlement	$32,463.60 p.a. *($624.30 each pfn)*
Interest on bank accounts & term deposits (@5%)	$18,500
Total	$50,963.60

> *Cash flow will still be positive and they will be able to meet the cost of living for both of them.*
>
> *However, assuming an 8% interest rate on the reverse mortgage, the amount owing has grown to around $270,000 by the end of year one and $372,000 by the end of year five.*

Chapter 20
Using a trust or company structure

For aged care purposes private trust and company structures are treated as per Centrelink's assessment process and you need to be aware that the Centrelink approach can be very different to the legal or tax treatment of a trust or company structure. Centrelink assesses trusts and companies against two tests: a source test and a control test.

Put simply, the source test asks the question, "where did the money/assets originate?" while the control test asks, "who controls (or could expect to control) the trust?"

Based on the outcomes of these tests, the asset value will be attributed to an individual or to a group of people in percentage terms and any income earned by the trust is attributed according to the same percentages. For example, a family trust that was established with funds from the parents with no contributions from the children and with the parents as trustees would be viewed as an assessable asset attributable to the parents.

It is important to seek legal advice about the establishment of a trust from someone who understands aged care and pension assessment. If the trust is established in such a way that the elderly person loses control of the asset and does not stand to benefit from the trust, the money can be considered a deprived asset/gift.

> *Look at it this way: with a private trust or company structure the asset is assessable but the income is not deemed as it is with other financial assets, instead actual taxable income is used. This can assist to "bridge the gap" between the asset test and the income test.*

A single homeowner can have $186,750 in assets but, assuming $176,750 was held in financial assets (with $10,000 for car, contents etc.), the deemed income would be $7,284.75. This would exceed the $3,900p.a. income threshold, reducing pension entitlement and increasing the income-tested fee. For a single non-homeowner—the majority of people living in aged care—the asset test increases to $321,750 while the income threshold remains the same. If $311,750 was held in financial assets, as is often the case following the sale of the former home and payment of the accommodation bond, the deemed income would be $13,359.75.

Using assets that would be subject to deeming—such as money in bank accounts or term deposits—to purchase an insurance bond within a family trust will mean you have the same level of assessable assets but less assessable income.

Tips and traps with this strategy:

- Payment from an insurance bond is tax free on the death of the life insured to the bond owner.
- Unexpected withdrawals can have a negative impact on your pension and on the income-tested fee and may also have tax consequences.
- Withdrawals can be structured to create a "pseudo annuity"—withdrawals from an insurance bond are pro-rata capital and income with only the income part assessed for social security/tax/aged care.
- **Couple**—have separate bonds/lives insured. Where an insurance bond is held jointly it will only pay on the death of the last survivor, becoming an asset of the survivor in the meantime. Depending on the estate planning, it may be better to have an insurance bond for each member of a couple and have the bond paid to the children/beneficiaries rather than the surviving spouse to protect pension entitlement (under the asset test).
- **Be aware of stamp duty**—stamp duty is payable on the monies used to establish an insurance bond. It may be best to establish the investment with a small amount and

add-on the remaining monies within the first year so as not to affect the 125% contribution limit.
- A family trust is a non-estate asset. You should always seek legal advice and beneficiaries of the trust should be considered in light of the will. The trust can distribute to the estate on death to ensure that beneficiaries of the will are not disinherited.

Case Study

Emma has already moved into aged care as a low care resident and has agreed to pay an accommodation bond of $300,000. She has decided to sell her house to fund her care. Following the sale and payment of the accommodation bond, Emma will be left with $320,000 in her bank account.

Her assets will be:

Bank accounts	$320,000
Accommodation bond	$300,000
Personal Effects	$2,000

Cost of care:

Daily care fee	$38.33
Income tested fee	$7.21
Total	$16,622.10
+ *chocolates, haircuts & outings*	$2,600
=	$19,222.10

Income:

Age pension	$14,046.30 *($540.24 each pfn)*
Interest	$16,000
Total	$29,983.80

Emma could use $250,000 of her cash assets to purchase an insurance bond within a family trust structure, leaving $70,000 in the bank (subject to deeming). The deemed income would be ($44,600@3%=$1,338+$25,400@4.5%=$1,143) $2,481 which is less than the income test threshold of $3,900. In addition, as Emma's total income would be less than $847.90pfn, no income tested fee would be payable. This would represent a saving of $1930.85 on her annual cost of care.

However, because the trust is an assessable asset, her pension entitlement would be calculated as follows:

$322,000−$321,750=$250   *asset above threshold*

$250 \times 1.5 \div 1000 = \$37.54$ *pension reduction from full pension*

Pension entitlement=$728.93 pfn

This represents an increase in pension entitlement of $4,905.81 p.a. Of course full pension entitlement could be achieved through the use of other asset reducing strategies such as gifting, pre-paying a funeral or purchasing a funeral bond. Such strategies may also need to be considered to maintain the same amount of pension entitlement in the future because the assets inside the trust will grow in a compound interest like environment.

While the savings in pension entitlement and income tested fees are attractive, they need to be weighed up against the cost of establishing a trust and paying tax within the insurance bond at 30¢ *(less deductions)*.

Establishing loan accounts through a trust may be a better alternative than gifting for people who wish to extend the use of money to their children but retain control over the asset.

Case Study

Elsie is 82 and has been assessed as requiring **Low Care**. She has been living with one of her daughters as well as receiving in-home care for nearly six months. During this time the family has decided that they cannot provide the care she needs and it would be best for her to move to an aged care facility close by. The home in which she used to live was re-zoned from rural to residential, creating a huge increase in the value of the land, and Elsie received $6 million on its sale.

Elsie's assets are:

House sold	$6,000,000
Cash	$50,000
Contents	$5,000

Cost of care:

Accommodation bond	$500,000
Daily care fee	$38.33 p.d.
Income tested fee	$64.69
Total	$37,602.30
+ *chocolates, haircuts & outings*	$2,600
=	$40,202.30

Income:

Pension	$0
Interest	$277,500
Total	$277,500

The outcome will be the same if Elsie retains the proceeds of the sale in deemed assets or gifts for five years.

Using a family trust wouldn't entitle Elsie to any more pension entitlement as the asset is still hers, but it would enable her to reduce her income-tested fee. Let's see how that works out.

House sold	$6,000,000
establishes family trust & loans $5m to children	
Cash	$550,000
Contents	$5,000

Cost of care:

Accommodation bond	$500,000
Daily care fee	$38.33 p.d.
Income tested fee	$3.92 p.d.
reduction $22,181.05p.a.	
Total	$15,421.25
+ chocolates, haircuts & outings	$2,600
	= $18,021.25

Income:

Pension	$0
Interest	$27,500
Total	$27,500

It should be noted that the same effect would be achieved if Elsie purchased an insurance bond instead of loaning money to her children. If Elsie reduced her cash by purchasing an insurance bond within a trust her income tested fee would further reduce.

There are costs involved in setting up trusts and they may incur ongoing accounting fees. In addition, the rules around their tax treatment are complex and can change—some changes were made in the *May 2011 Budget* for example—so we must stress that you seek legal advice on your particular situation and ensure that your adviser is versed in trusts as they relate to aged care and pension entitlements.

Chapter 21
Annuities & other income streams

The purchase of annuities for pension and aged care purposes used to be a valuable strategy as complying annuities had a 100% or 50% asset test exemption (depending on when they were purchased) and were 100% exempt from the calculation of the accommodation bond. Unfortunately, there is no longer an asset test exemption—social security or aged care—that is applied to annuities purchased after 20 September 2007. However, an annuity is a very simple and secure investment with favourable income assessment from a social security and aged care income tested fee perspective.

Annuities are generally classified into two classes:

- **Lifetime Annuities**—pay a known amount of income from the start date until the investor dies
- **Fixed Term Annuities**—are split into short-term (up to five years) and long-term (more than six years or less if life expectancy is less) and each pay a known amount for the fixed term.

There are a number of different payment options from annuities. The first is whether the payments will be comprised of capital and income, with the capital being reduced to $0 at the end of the term. This is known as Nil Residual Capital Value (RCV0). The other is where the investment value is preserved and only the income is paid to the investor (RCV100).

Obviously the first produces a much higher cash flow as the principal is being paid out over the term. For example, a $100,000 annuity earning 6% over six years with a nil RCV will produce a cash flow of $22,666 per year, while the same annuity with RCV100 would produce $6,000. Importantly, the amount of assessable income is the same for each as the return of capital (known as the deductible amount) is not considered income.

The timing of payments from the annuity can be as regular as monthly or as a once-a-year payment and you can index the payments up to about 8%, meaning less income will be received in the short term and more in the latter stages.

Annuities can be purchased using investment funds or from superannuation.

Annuity strategies are often considered for the use of monies coming from the sale of the former home in excess of the accommodation bond. They generally receive a favourable income assessment because the money that is returned to you is a combination of the principal you invested and the income earned.

Some key points regarding the use of annuity strategies:

- All annuities are fixed interest investments. While this provides certainty of payment over

the term, if interest rates go up you may have been better off not investing.
- The value of the annuity forms part of the assessable assets for calculating the amount of accommodation bond or accommodation charge payable. However, accessing a lump sum may cause significant exit penalties.
- Short-term annuities (less than five years or life expectancy) are not assessed based on the income above the deductible amount—they are simply deemed to earn income as a bank account would be.
- Long-term annuities (six years or more or life expectancy) are often preferred due to the favourable Centrelink and aged care treatment. However, you should consider the implications of the person passing away inside the term of the annuity. For people with a short life expectancy, the value of purchasing the annuity—in terms of increased pension and reduced aged care costs—may be outweighed by the exit penalty. This effect is often compounded by a number of other factors. Because the amount of money invested is normally significant, generally as a result of the sale of the former home, the term and the indexation are increased to reduce the amount of assessable income.

- Increasing the term and indexation can produce higher amounts of pension entitlement and reduced aged care costs in the short term. However, exit penalties are based on the calculation of net present value. Net present value is simply today's value of all future cash flows. Increasing the term and the indexation means that the life company has been promised more money for longer and will generally create a higher exit penalty unless interest rates have dropped significantly.
- Depending on the increases in the income threshold for pension and aged care, indexing the annuity too high may lead to an increase in the reduction of pension and increase in aged care costs than if the indexation was lower.
- Annuities can often generate more cash flow than is spent. The unspent income can increase the value of deemed assets such as bank accounts.

Case Study

Judy is aged 83 and has recently sold her home to fund an accommodation bond of $350,000. She had $270,000 left in her bank accounts. As a result, her pension has reduced by $145.79pfn and she is paying a small income tested fee of $5.92p.d. Her cash flow is more than sufficient in meeting her cost of care, however, she has heard that an annuity may benefit her pension and aged care cost.

If she keeps $20,000 in cash and uses $250,000 to purchase a six-year annuity she will receive $46,142p.a., of which $4,475.33 would be assessed as income. Her pension would increase by $123.19pfn/$3,202.94p.a. and her income tested fee would reduce to $0 (a saving of $2,160.80).

However, the high level of unspent cash flow will quickly build up in her bank accounts, reducing her pension and increasing the income tested fee. Strategies such as gifting or pre-paying funeral expenses can be used to lower the deemed assets but are unlikely to be enough to increase the pension and reduce aged care costs at the desired levels.

If Judy extended the term to 15 years her annual payment would reduce to $22,724 and the assessable income would be $6,057p.a. (a large part of the growth in the income component is the higher interest rates currently being paid for longer terms). Compared with her current situation her pension would increase by $92.77pfn/$2,412.02p.a. and her income tested fee would be reduced to $0 (a saving of $2,493.40). Because the cash flow is significantly less than with the six-year annuity, her pension decrease and cost of care increases would be delayed.

If she took a lifetime annuity (indexed at CPI) $20,351.81 would be paid in the first year, with future annual payments being this amount (indexed at CPI) for the rest of her life. Assuming there are no commutations, the deductible amount would be $30,560 each year, meaning that none of the payment would be assessable until it exceeds $30,560p.a. Her pension would increase to full entitlement of $729.30pfn (an increase of $145.79pfn/$3,790.54p.a. over her current situation) and no income tested fee would be payable (a saving of $2,160.80).

Chapter 22

Why pay a bigger accommodation bond?

While it defies most people's logic to pay more than you need to as an accommodation bond, for some people this can be a very simple but effective strategy.

Many facilities will offer discounts on fees and charges to residents who wish to pay more than the market price or negotiated amount of accommodation bond. Facilities may offer a particular discount arrangement, i.e. if you pay an extra $150,000 in accommodation bond they will waive the retention fee or they may offer the discount to you as a percentage, i.e. provide you with a discount on your fees and charges of 4% for any additional bond paid. In this case it is common for the facility to state that they only accept additional amounts in lump sums of $50,000 or $100,000.

At its optimum this strategy can achieve a triple benefit for the resident: a discount on their fees and charges, an increase in their pension entitlement and a reduction in the daily income tested fee. Like many financial strategies this benefit will not be received by everyone to the same extent or even for the same person beyond a certain point. This strategy can be particularly valuable to residents who choose extra services, as generating income to pay the extra service fee may create or increase the income tested fee.

Bear in mind that the income tested fee is often not included in the fees and charges that you can negotiate with the aged care facility because it is a fee calculated by the Department of Health and Ageing after the resident enters care and reviewed quarterly. This fee could be anything between $0 and $64.69p.d. and will be used by the government to offset its own funding on a dollar for dollar basis. As such, the facility has no way of knowing how much income tested fee a resident is going to pay and whether this is likely to change. Similarly, the resident, through the restructuring of their assets, may reduce their liability to pay an income tested fee and so there would be no real benefit in negotiating costs that include this fee.

Key points to consider

If you are contemplating paying a bigger accommodation bond, you must first determine the total rate of return being achieved and how this compares with other investments, with consideration for the risk/return trade-off.

To achieve the best return possible it is important to be aware that you can go too far. To maximise your return you will need to determine the point at which the pension is maximised and the daily income tested fee is minimised, as the discount being provided by the facility is constant. Giving capital beyond this point will mean that your total return is reducing because no more pension can be received or the income tested fee cannot be reduced further (or is $0) and the only return on your capital beyond this point is the discount from the facility. While this seems logical and perhaps you think we are stating the obvious, it is not always clear when looking at the numbers and often requires some trial and error to get the amount right.

The discount that you agree to with the facility will be reflected in the Residential Care Agreement (RCA) that you sign on entry. Because the discount rate is set at the date of permanent entry, it is very much like entering into a fixed interest investment: if interest rates go up then potentially you are worse off than if you invested the money in a cash fund, but if interest rates go down then potentially you are better off.

There is no set formula for determining the discount a facility will provide. It is going to depend on a number of factors including whether the money can be used to offset interest on or reduce debt or whether it will be earning interest on deposit; the tax treatment of the income produced/offset; the facility management's view on likely changes to interest rates during the period of residence and their experience/willingness to undertake such agreements. Some of the larger groups will have a central office to handle preparation of the RCA and any negotiations, or they may have a stated discount rate for their facilities, while others may leave the negotiations to the discretion of the facility manager/owner or their advisers.

Case Studies

Pensioner and war widow (not exceeding asset test)

Isobel is an age pensioner entering Low Care.

Her assets are:

House	$600,000
Bank accounts	$50,000
Personal effects	$2,000

The facility has set her accommodation bond at $350,000, offering a 4% discount for amounts paid above this.

If Isobel pays the $350,000 bond, **her cost of care will be:**

Daily care fee	$38.33 p.d.
Income tested fee	$6.69 p.d.
Total	$16,432.30
+ *chocolates, haircuts & outings*	$2,600 p.a.
	= $19,032.30

Retention will be deducted from the bond at $318 per month for a maximum of five years.

Income:

Pension	$14,496.30 p.a. *($557.55 pfn)*
Interest	$15,000
Total	$29,496.30 p.a.

Isobel is allowed to have $321,750 in assets but can only earn $3,900p.a. in income before her pension reduces. Her pension is unaffected by the asset test and is being reduced due to the income test.

If Isobel kept $50,000 in her bank account and paid an accommodation bond of $600,000 (effectively exchanging the value of her home for the bond), a discount of $10,000 would be applied to her daily care fee and **her cost of care will be:**

Daily care fee	$12.85 p.d.
Income tested fee	$0 p.d.
Total	$4,691.25
+ *chocolates, haircuts & outings*	$2,600
=	$7,291.25

Income:

Pension	$18,961.80 p.a. *($729.30 pfn)*
Interest	$2,500 p.a.
Total	$21,461.80 p.a.

The effective rate of return to Isobel for the additional bond is 6%.

War widow (with no qualifying service)
Let's look at another example to see how different pensions impact on the efficiency of the strategy:

Betty wants to move to the same facility as Isobel and wishes tosell her home to pay her bond.

Betty's assets are:

Home	$900,000
Cash	$75,000
Personal effects	$2,000

If Betty moves to the same facility as Isobel, paying the $350,000 bond, **her cost of care will be:**

Accommodation bond	$350,000	
Daily care fee	$38.33	
Income tested fee	$29.77	p.d.
Total	$24,856.60	p.a.
+ *chocolates, haircuts & outings*	$2,600	p.a.
=	$27,456.60	

Income:

War Widows Pension	$19,206.20 p.a.	*($738.70 pfn)*
Income support supplement	$0	
Interest	$31,250	p.a.
Total	$50,456.20	p.a.

If Betty paid $900,000 as an accommodation bond the discount that the facility would apply is $22,000. However, the maximum discount Betty can receive is the cost of her care fees:

(Daily care fee $13,990.45+Retention $3,816=$17,806.45)

Her cost of care will be:

Daily care fee	$0	p.d.
Income tested fee	$7.08	p.d.
Total	$3,018.55	p.a.
+ *chocolates, haircuts & outings*	$2,600	p.a.
=	$5,618.55	p.a.

Income:

War Widows Pension	$19,206.20 p.a.	*($738.70 pfn)*
Income support supplement	$5,740.80 p.a.	*($220.80 pfn)*
Interest	$3,750 p.a.	
Total	$28,697.00 p.a.	

The effective rate of return on the additional bond for Betty is 5%.

Betty will always have an income tested fee applied to her as her War Widows Pension and income support supplement exceed the income tested fee threshold.

In both these case studies the resident could have achieved the same pension and income tested fee outcome by using a company or family trust structure (and purchasing non-income producing assets), or purchasing a holiday home (with no rent received) or a vacant block of land. However, each of these strategies has costs associated with establishing, maintaining and/or sale.

If you are considering paying more as an accommodation bond and looking at the

rate of return being achieved, you should also take into account the simplicity of the strategy's establishment and management, the fact that the amount paid (less any retentions) is guaranteed by the government and that the money is payable within a short time of leaving the facility (refer to refunding the accommodation bond in Chapter 16).

Case Study

Beryl is 85 and has been assessed as requiring High Care. The aged care facility has quoted an accommodation bond of $500,000, and offered to discount the extra service fee by 4% if she chooses to pay a higher bond. Beryl's house is expected to sell for $1 million after costs.

If Beryl sells her house and pays the standard bond her assets will be:

Cash	$600,000
Contents	$5,000

Cost of care:

Accommodation bond	$500,000	
Daily care fee	$38.33	p.d.
Extra service fee	$40	p.d.
Income tested fee	$14.43	p.d.
Total	$34,222.40	
+ *chocolates, haircuts & outings*	$2,600	p.a.
=	$36,822.40	

Income:

Pension	$7,746.18	p.a.
Interest	$30,000	
Total	$37,746.18	p.a.

If Beryl paid an accommodation bond of $1 million

Keeping $100,000 in deemed assets

Contents	$5,000

Cost of care:

Accommodation bond	$1million	
Daily care fee	$40.25 p.d.	*increase $700.89*
Extra service fee	$0 p.d.	
Income tested fee	$0 p.d.	*reduction $5,266.95*
Total	$14,691.25	
+ *chocolates, haircuts & outings*	$2,600	p.a.
=	$17,291.25	p.a.

Income:

Pension	$18,961.80 p.a.	*increase $11,215.50*
Interest	$5,000	
Total	$23,961.80 p.a.	

This equates to a return of 6%.

> When considering such a strategy it is important to consider all the factors we have mentioned above. It is also important to be aware that if you need to access some of your bond at a later time the facility can charge you interest on the amount that is refunded to you. The maximum interest rate is based on the Maximum Permissible Interest Rate (MPIR) on the date you entered care as a permanent resident; for people who entered care between 1 July and 30 September 2011 the MPIR is 9%.

Chapter 23

When to go it alone

In Chapter 13 we told you about the assets assessment process which determines the maximum amount of accommodation bond or accommodation charge payable. You start the process by filling out what is commonly known as "the blue book" and the accompanying information booklet has a section titled "The timing of your assets assessment" which explains that if a resident completes the asset assessment prior to entry, their assets will be assessed at the time the assessment is undertaken. If the assessment is completed after you enter care, then your assets will be assessed as at the date of permanent entry.

What's so significant about that? The answer is: a great deal. As you read earlier, the timing of an asset assessment can create very different outcomes when dealing with a couple. It's worth repeating the key points:

- A couple who both enter care on the same day and submit to the asset assessment after they enter will each have 50% of the value of the former home assessed in their assets.
- A couple who enter care on separate days and submit their assets assessment after entry

to care will have the value of the home exempted from the first to enter and half assessed against the second.
- A couple who both complete the assets assessment prior to entering care will both declare that the spouse lives in the home, thereby exempting the home from each in the assets assessment.

Assets assessments for people who have not yet entered permanent care are valid for up to 4 months, meaning residents could enter care on separate days but as the assessment was carried out prior to entry, the home would remain exempt.

While it may seem attractive to you (as a couple) to undertake the assessment prior to entry and minimise the amount of accommodation payment, careful consideration should be given to such a strategy.

Whether or not to undertake the asset assessment at all and the timing of the assessment will depend on what the chosen facility will accept and what your intentions are for your former home.

Because the supported resident supplement and the accommodation charge are equivalent, it is not uncommon for facilities to have a preference for a high care supported resident to assist them in meeting their ratios. If you choose a high care bed with extra services, you will have to pay an accommodation bond and a supported resident would not be accepted as no supplement is payable to the facility. Many aged care facilities will require an asset assessment for a supported resident to be provided prior to or on entry. If you are not claiming to be supported you will pay either the maximum accommodation charge or a negotiated amount of accommodation bond.

Whether you wish to keep and rent or sell the former home will also be a key consideration in determining whether or not to submit to an asset assessment and the timing of the assessment.

The timing of an asset assessment so that no accommodation payment is required from either member of a couple may seem attractive and logical for people wishing to retain the former home. It is important to remember, (as discussed in Chapter 18), that fully supported residents do not meet the criteria to have the asset and income exemptions applied to the home. Where only one person is liable to pay an accommodation payment which is going to be used to meet the exemption criteria, careful consideration needs to be given to the impact of that person pre-deceasing the other in terms of pension entitlement, cost of care and cash flow positions.

Case Study

George (High Care) and Beryl (Low Care) both currently live in their own home with assistance being provided through care packages and family support. They have decided that they would like to move into an aged care facility that is close by.

House	$400,000
Cash	$60,000
Contents	$5,000

If they both enter care on the same day with the asset assessment completed after admission, each person will have $232,500 in assessable assets. If they both submit to the asset assessment prior to admission, their assessable assets would be $32,500 each.

George's asset assessment (on or after admission) will indicate that he is ineligible to be a supported resident and will need to pay $30.55p.d. accommodation charge. Beryl's assessment will also state that she is ineligible to be supported and the maximum bond she can be asked to pay is $193,500.

If George enters first and submits an asset assessment after entry (or if only George submits to the assessment prior to entry), the asset assessment will show that George's assessable assets are $32,500 which is less than the minimum assets amount of $39,000 so no accommodation charge is payable (a saving of $30.55p.d./$11,150.75p.a.). If Beryl enters first and submits an asset assessment after entry (or if only Beryl submits to the assessment prior to entry) then her assessable assets would be $32,500 and no accommodation bond would be payable. George's assessable assets would be $232,500 and the maximum accommodation charge would be payable.

If Beryl submits to an asset assessment after George has entered care the maximum accommodation bond she can be asked to pay is still $193,500. The assets of the couple are always split on a 50/50 basis—you cannot "load up" assets from one to another.

However, because Beryl is not going to be eligible to be a supported resident, careful consideration needs to be given to the advantages of undertaking the assessment. Obviously, undertaking the assessment means that the amount of bond Beryl can pay is known and this sum of $193,500 may be less than the market price. If Beryl cannot pay the market price bond it may restrict her access to the care of her choice, as she would need to find a facility that is willing to accept a bond of $193,500.

From Beryl's point of view (or that of her adviser) she may wish to negotiate to pay a higher bond in exchange for a discount on her fees. This strategy may also provide other benefits including an increase in pension and a reduced income tested fee. If George pre-deceases her, the higher bond/fee discount strategy may also provide Beryl with a higher pension and lower income tested fee in the future. However, if she undertakes the asset assessment and provides this to the aged care facility, they cannot accept a higher bond than the amount stated, even if she offers to pay one.

> *As this case study highlights, there are many possible outcomes for George and Beryl depending on the timing of their asset assessment which can impact on their pension entitlement, their cost of care, eligibility to keep and rent their former home with asset and income exemptions applying, and their ability to afford care in the short and long term. The paramount consideration remains, however, their ability to access the care of their choice.*

Chapter 24

Better to give & receive

The sale of your home can mean that you have more liquid funds at your disposal than ever before. The move to aged care can also prompt a desire to enable your children to "inherit now" by allowing them to influence the way in which the money is spent. Or you might decide to give money to people that are not in your will (often grandchildren) to minimise any later disputes about the distribution of funds.

A common question is "How much money can I give away?" The simple answer is "As much as you want". The government cannot stop you from giving all (or none) of your money away. However, you should be aware of how gifting can affect your pension and cost of care.

On Budget Night 2006 the rules around gifting for aged care were brought in line with the social security rules around gifting (deprived assets). Prior to this, assessable assets only included those assets in existence at the date of permanent entry.

People entering care after 1 January 2007 should be aware that any gift in excess of $10,000 in a financial year and $30,000 over five years immediately prior to entering aged care will be assessed as an asset and deemed to earn income.

This assessment will impact on the calculation of:
- Pension entitlement under both the asset and income test
- Assessable assets for determining Supported Resident status
- Assessable assets for determining the maximum accommodation bond or accommodation charge
- The deemed income on the gift will be counted in assessable income for determining the amount of income tested fee.

Gifting within the allowed amounts can be a great strategy (often used in conjunction with other asset reduction strategies such as pre-paying a funeral or purchasing a funeral bond) to assist people who are slightly over the supported resident thresholds of $39,000 or $102,544.

Accessing care may be easier if you are classified as a supported resident rather than someone who doesn't have the capacity to pay a market price bond. For high care residents needing to pay an accommodation charge, the standard daily care fee and the accommodation charge is equivalent to 137% of the full pension, making care unaffordable. As a supported resident, you pay part or none of the accommodation charge and the government picks up the tab for the balance.

However, gifting to reduce your capacity to pay a market price bond may make accessing care harder so it is always important to check what the facility will accept. Careful consideration needs to be given to reducing your assets below the $39,000 threshold if the former home is being retained, as fully supported residents don't meet the asset and income exemption criteria. This can also be an important consideration for a couple where one is entering care and the other is remaining in the home. In the event that the person living in the home were to pre-decease the person in care, the person living in care may wish to take advantage of the asset and income exemptions to keep and rent the home.

The allowable gifting amount of $10,000 per financial year is relatively small and may not be sufficient. It may be necessary to look at timing the gifts to be around the end of financial year, e.g. a gift of $10,000 on 30 June and a gift of

$10,000 on 1 July would reduce the assessable assets by $20,000 in a few days.

If you are contemplating the idea of gifting above the limits, do bear in mind the potential impact on your ability to access and afford care. Life expectancy has to be taken into account in weighing up the detriment (reduced pension, increased cost of care) against the potential benefits that will be received in five years from the date of the gift.

Loaning money to children through a trust may be a better option—while the asset will always be assessable, income is assessed on the actual income received only and you can retain control over the monies and have them paid back in the event that you need them or feel that the money is being spent unwisely.

Case Study

June has recently been assessed as requiring High Care. Her son has lived with her for the past seven years to support his mother and is receiving a carer's pension, so the home is exempted from her assessable assets.

House	$500,000	*(exempt)*
Cash	$100,000	
Contents	$2,000	

Cost of care:

Daily care fee	$40.25	p.d.
Accommodation charge	$30.29	p.d.
Total	$25,746.54	
+ *chocolates, haircuts & outings*	$2,600	p.a.
=	$28,346.54	

Income:

Pension	$18,961.80	p.a.
Interest	$5,000	
Total	$23,961.80	
Cash flow deficit	$4,384.74	p.a.

June is eligible to be a partially supported resident but she is unable to meet her cost of care from her pension and investments.

She is eligible to keep and rent her home because she is paying an accommodation charge. She may need to consider renting the home to her son or drawing some of her capital each year to meet her cash flow shortfall.

If she rents the home to her son he may be eligible to receive rent assistance of up to $116.40pfn, depending on the amount of rent he pays. A nominal rent would ensure that the home and the rental income would be exempt for as long as June is paying the accommodation charge.

Let's look at the impact of gifting $10,000 on 30 June and $10,000 on 1 July (prior to an asset assessment) on June's **cost of care:**

House	$500,000	*(exempt)*
Cash	$80,000	
Contents	$2,000	

Cost of care:

Daily care fee	$40.25	p.d.
Accommodation charge	$20.67	p.d.
Total	$22,237	
+ *chocolates, haircuts & outings*	$2,600	p.a.
=	$24,837	

Income:

Pension	$18,961.80	p.a.
Interest	$4,000	
Total	$22,961.80	
Cash flow deficit	$1,875.20	p.a.

As we can see, June still has a cash flow deficit but it has been greatly reduced.

Chapter 25

Meeting funeral costs

Organising your own funeral may not sound like a whole lot of fun but it can be a very sensible decision, both financially and emotionally.

In arranging a funeral there are many decisions to be made. Where should it be held? Burial or cremation? Should the service be conducted by a church minister, celebrant or a family member or friend? Will there be a casket? What music do you want? Flowers or donations to charities? Who should give the eulogies or carry the casket? Are there special religious or cultural beliefs or customs that need to be observed? All these decisions and more will be faced by the person responsible for arranging the funeral and a pre-paid funeral means that the answers to these questions—your wishes—are already known. And a pre-paid funeral also means that the financial arrangements have already been taken care of.

Pre-paying a funeral or purchasing a funeral bond

A funeral bond provides a lump sum to assist in meeting the costs of a funeral. A pre-paid funeral means that the cost of the specific funeral for that individual is met upfront (often years before the person has passed away).

A funeral bond is essentially an investment (normally capital guaranteed or very conservatively invested) that you make with a life insurance company to assist in meeting the cost of your funeral when that day comes. There is no maximum limit for a funeral bond as such but obviously you should only invest an amount that you anticipate will meet your funeral costs. The maximum for the purposes of asset and income test exemptions is $11,250. The money earned by the investment will have tax paid by the life company, with the net amount added to your investment as what is often called a "bonus" or a "declared bonus". The full amount of your initial investment plus the bonuses will be paid to your estate or to your nominated funeral director.

Pre-paying a funeral or purchasing a funeral bond is often considered in conjunction with gifting to reduce assessable assets.

Here are the key points to consider in purchasing a pre-paid funeral or a funeral bond:

- The asset and income test exemption for funeral bonds is limited to $11,250
- The asset and income test exemptions for a prepaid funeral is unlimited (up to the cost)
- Pre-paid funerals can include very expensive items, such as purchase of a plot, headstone or plaque and casket, as well as other items
- Funeral bonds generate low returns when compared with the inflation on funerals. As such there is a risk that, even if the bond covers likely expenses at time of purchase, bond proceeds may fall short of the amount needed when the time comes.
- Where the purchase of a funeral bond or pre-paid funeral is to reduce assessable assets, one may exempt more assets than the other.

Case Study

Remember June in Chapter 24 who gifted $20,000 to reduce her assessable assets? If she also pre-pays a funeral for $30,000, her cost of care will be:

House	$500,000	*(exempt)*
Cash	$50,000	
Prepaid funeral	$30,000	
Contents	$2,000	

Cost of care:

Daily care fee	$40.25	p.d.
Accommodation charge	$6.25	p.d.
Total	$16,972.50	
+ *chocolates, haircuts & outings*	$2,600	p.a.
=	$19,572.50	

Income:

Pension	$18,961.80	p.a.
Interest	$2,500	
Total	$21,461.80	
Cash flow surplus	$1,889.30	p.a.

June's accommodation charge has reduced significantly but because she still pays a charge, she is eligible to keep and rent the home with an asset and income exemption applied. If June reduced her assessable assets below $39,000 and no accommodation charge was payable, the two year general exemption would be applied to the former home.

SECTION 5

Appendix

In tackling the aged care maze there are a number of resources and tools that you may find handy and in this section we have listed some of the most important. Here you'll find government services including websites that provide information such as how to get in contact with your local ACAT Team, the latest aged care fees and charges, and contact points for carer's payments and allowances. We also provide you with more specific services such as those available to people in rural and regional areas, culturally appropriate care and services provided through the Department of Veterans' Affairs to veterans and war widows and widowers. The resources also cover non-government services, such as online directories for aged care services, retirement village directories and placement agents.

As part of the directory we have given you a quick guide on how to use the online directories to search for aged care services and retirement villages that suit you.

If you have already started on the voyage of identifying aged care choices for you or a loved one you will know that there are many special terms and acronyms to come to grips with. So last but certainly not least in our appendix section is a glossary explaining the terms, phrases and acronyms in this book which can also assist you in your conversations with service providers.

Please bear in mind that the information in this section is by no means an exhaustive list of every service that may be available to you; it is simply designed to get you started.

Resources

Aged Care Australia

Aged Care Australia is the Australian Government's entry point to ageing and aged care information. The website covers the spectrum of aged care, including help to stay at home, finding a facility, FAQs and useful contacts. Probably the most useful feature is the ACAT finder, where you can enter your suburb or postcode and find details of your local ACAT Team.
Website: www.agedcareaustralia.gov.au

Aged Care Complaints Investigation Scheme

The Aged Care Complaints Investigation Scheme is a free service which investigates concerns about any aspect of an Australian Government subsidised aged care service.
Phone: 1800-550-552
Website: www.agedcarecomplaints.govspace.gov.au
(includes access to an online complaints form)

Postal address: Aged Care Complaints Investigation Scheme c/– Department of Health and Ageing GPO Box 9848 in your Capital City.

Aged Care Commissioner

If you have made a complaint to the Aged Care Complaints Investigation Scheme and you are unhappy with the Scheme's decision or the way it has handled your complaint, you can make a complaint to the Office of the Aged Care Commissioner.
Phone: 1800-500-294
Email: info@agedcarecommissioner.net.au
Website: www.agedcarecommissioner.net.au
Postal address: The Aged Care Commissioner Locked Bag 3 Collins Street East Melbourne VIC 8003

Aged Care Fees & Charges

Up-to-date information on the Schedule of Resident Fees and Charges for Aged Care is available on the Department of Health and Ageing website. This includes information such as the amount of daily care fees, income tested fee thresholds, interest rates on unpaid accommodation bonds and charges, maximum accommodation charges and retention amounts.

Website: www.health.gov.au
(Write "Fees & Charges" in the search box to be taken to the relevant page which is updated regularly.)

Carer Payments and Allowances

Some carers may be eligible for a Carer Payment or Carer Allowance from Centrelink.
Phone: 13 27 17
Website: www.centrelink.gov.au

Commonwealth Respite and Carelink Centres

Commonwealth Respite and Carelink Centres provide information face to face or by phone about available aged care or disability services. They can also assist carers with options to take a break through short-term and emergency respite services and provide advice on and coordinate access to respite services in a carer's local area.
Phone: 1800-052-222.

Deaf, hearing impaired or speech impaired callers may call through the National Relay Service using their modem or TTY by dialing 1800-555-677 then asking for 1800-052-222. Speech impaired callers may also call through Speech-to-Speech Relay by dialing 1800-555-727 then asking for the freecall 1800 number.

Alzheimer's Australia including National Dementia Helpline

The Australian Government funds the National Dementia Helpline, a telephone and support service staffed by trained and experienced advisers at Alzheimer's Australia.
Phone: 1800-100-500

The Alzheimer's Australia website provides help sheets, research and publications about dementia as well as details about services and support in each state and territory.
Website: www.alzheimers.org.au

REGIONAL & RURAL SERVICES

Australian Government Regional Information Service (AGRIS)

AGRIS brings together a number of practical ways to help you get information about Australian Government programs and services. It is made up of an information line and a website.
Phone: 1800-026-222

Website: www.regionalaustralia.gov.au

Farmer Assistance Line

This is a special service for farmers provided by Centrelink. The calls are directed to rural call centres and staff can provide advice on a range of programs including farmers' eligibility for Centrelink payments and services.
Phone: 1800-050-585
Website: www.centrelink.gov.au

Rural Health Information Line

The Rural Health information line covers Australian Government rural health programs and services.
Phone: 1800-020-787
Email: ruralhealth@health.gov.au
Website: www.health.gov.au/ruralhealth
Postal address: Rural Health Services and Policy Branch (MDP 91) Office of Rural Health Primary and Ambulatory Care Division Department of Health and Ageing GPO Box 9848 Canberra ACT 2601

CULTURALLY APPROPRIATE CARE

Partners in Culturally Appropriate Care (PICAC) Program

PICAC works with service providers, ethnic communities and the Department of Health and Ageing to ensure that the special needs of older people from culturally and linguistically diverse backgrounds are addressed. This initiative provides cross-cultural training and information sessions and encourages ethnic communities to form partnerships with aged care service providers in order to establish more culturally appropriate facilities.

Phone the Commonwealth Respite and Carelink Centre on 1800-052-222 or the relevant PICAC office:
- Queensland (07)3846-1099
- New South Wales (02)9378-1378
- Victoria (03)8823-7900
- Tasmania (03)6221-0999
- South Australia (08)8241-9900
- Western Australia (08)9381-0660
- Northern Territor (08)8941-1004
- Australian Capital Territory (02)6205-1302

Australian Multicultural Foundation (AMF) and the Royal Melbourne Institute of Technology (RMIT)

These institutions have developed dementia resources for carers from culturally and linguistically diverse backgrounds. Copies of these audiotapes are available from the Aged Care Information Line on 1800-500-853.

HOME & COMMUNITY CARE

New South Wales

Department of Ageing, Disability and Home Care
Level 5, 83 Clarence Street, Sydney NSW 2000
Phone: (02)8270-2000
TTY: (02)8270-2167 (for people who are deaf)
Email: info@dadhc.nsw.gov.au

Victoria

Department of Health
50 Lonsdale Street, Melbourne, VIC 3000
Phone: 1300-650-172 (local call fee within Victoria, except mobile phones) (61 3)9096-0000 (Interstate, international and mobile callers)

Queensland

Disability and Community Care Services
Level 6B, Neville Bonner Building, 75 William Street, Brisbane QLD 4000
Postal address: Disability Services GPO Box 806 Brisbane QLD 4001
Phone: 1800-177-120 (cost of a local call)
TTY: (07)3896-3471
Email: disabilityinfo@disability.qld.gov.au

South Australia

Office for the Ageing
Level 4SW, Riverside Centre, North Tce, Adelaide SA 5000
Postal address: PO Box 70 Rundle Mall Adelaide SA 5000
Phone: (08)8207 0522
Fax: (08)8207-0555
Email: ofta@dfc.sa.gov.au

Western Australia

Department of Health
189 Royal Street, East Perth WA 6004

Postal address: PO Box 8172 Perth Business Centre Perth WA 6849
Phone: (08)9222-4222

Tasmania

Department of Health and Human Services
34 Davey Street, Hobart TAS 7000
Phone: 1300-769-699
Fax: 1300-721-611
Email: mail@tascarepoint.net
Postal address: Home and Community Care Unit GPO Box 125 Hobart TAS 7001

Northern Territory

Department of Health and Families
87 Mitchell Street, Darwin, NT 0800
Postal address: PO Box 40596 Casuarina NT 0811
Phone: (08)8920-3700

Australian Capital Territory

ACT Health
11 Moore Street, Canberra City ACT 2601

Postal address: GPO Box 825 Canberra City
ACT 2601
Phone: (02)6205 1526

PUBLIC GUARDIANSHIP BOARDS

Guardianship issues may arise during the course of an aged care assessment. To find out more about guardianship, contact the relevant agency.

Australian Capital Territory

Office of the Community Advocate
Phone: (02)6207-0707
Email: oca@act.gov.au
Web: www.oca.act.gov.au

New South Wales

The NSW Public Guardian
Phone: (02)9265-3184 (Sydney)
(02)9671-9800 (Blacktown)
(02)4320-4888 (Gosford)
Email: informationsupport@opg.nsw.gov.au
Web: www.lawlink.nsw.gov.au/opg

Queensland

The Adult Guardian
Phone: (07)3234-0870
Email: adult.guardian@justice.qld.gov.au
Web: www.justice.qld.gov.au/91.htm

Victoria

Office of the Public Advocate
Phone: (03)9603-9500
Email: publicadvocate@justice.vic.gov.au
Web: www.publicadvocate.vic.gov.au

Tasmania

Office of the Public Guardian
Phone: (03)6233-7608
Email: public.guardian@info.tas.gov.au
Web: www.publicguardian.tas.gov.au

South Australia

Office of the Public Advocate
Phone: (08)8269-7575
Email: opasa@opa.sa.gov.au
Web: www.opa.sa.gov.au

Northern Territory

Office of Adult Guardianship
Phone: (08)8922-7116 (Darwin Public Guardian)
(08)8951-6739 (Alice Springs Public Guardian)
Web: www.nt.gov.au/justice/graphpages/

Western Australia

The Public Advocate
Phone: (08)9278-7300
Email: *(via online form on web)*
Web: www.justice.wa.gov.au

DEPARTMENT OF VETERANS' AFFAIRS (DVA)

Veterans' Home Care (VHC)

The Veterans' Home Care Program provides a range of services for eligible veterans and war widows and widowers. Following a VHC assessment, services such as domestic assistance, personal care, limited home and garden maintenance and respite care may be provided. The VHC assessment agency may also provide referrals, with the person's consent, to other government programs and community agencies best placed to meet specific needs.

To arrange a VHC assessment, call 1300-550-450 (local call). For general enquiries, call 13-32-54 (local call) or visit the Department of Veterans' Affairs (DVA) website.

Attendant Allowance (DVA)

An attendant allowance may be paid to veterans who suffer from specific service-related disabilities and, as a result, require continuous and permanent assistance for everyday activities such as dressing, feeding, bathing and toileting. This allowance is available where a veteran is living at home or in a community setting and is not being cared for at public expense. Attendant Allowance is not payable if Centrelink is paying a Carer Payment (formerly Carer's Pension). However, a Carer Allowance (formerly Domiciliary Nursing Care Benefit) paid by Centrelink does not prevent the payment of Attendant Allowance.

Phone: 13-32-54 (local call)
1800-555-254 (regional areas free call)

Community Nursing

DVA community nursing services are available to eligible veterans and war widows and widowers to meet assessed clinical and/or

personal care needs on referral from a general practitioner, treating doctor or specialist in hospital, hospital discharge planner or VHC assessment agency. Services are provided in the person's home.
Phone: 13-32-54 (local call)
1800-550-457 (regional areas)

HomeFront (DVA)

HomeFront is a preventive program to reduce falls and accidents in the home. It provides eligible members of the veteran community with a comprehensive assessment of their home environment, financial assistance towards the cost of recommended aids and appliances and information about DVA and community support services. Gold and White Card holders are eligible for HomeFront assistance once each calendar year.
Phone: 1800-801-945

Rehabilitation Appliances Program (RAP)

The Rehabilitation Appliances Program (RAP) helps eligible members of the veteran community minimise the impact of disabilities and assists them in caring for themselves and undertaking

everyday activities. The aids and appliances available range from mobility aids such as walking frames and wheelchairs, to continence products and visual aids. Specialists (e.g. occupational therapists, physiotherapists and nurses) assess a person's clinical need for aids and appliances through RAP. A local doctor or other relevant health professional can arrange a referral to RAP.
Phone: 13-32-54 (local call)
1800-550-457 (regional areas)

Recreational Transport Allowance (DVA)

This allowance provides financial assistance to veterans for transport for recreational purposes. It may be payable to veterans who have specific severe disabilities accepted as service-related. The rate payable is determined by the individual veteran's accepted disabilities.
Phone: 13-32-54 (local call)
1800-550-457 (regional areas)

NON-GOVERNMENT RESOURCES

Aged Care Online

www.agedcareonline.com.au is a non-government online directory of aged care services. It includes residential aged care, home and community care services and a step-by-step guide to assist users in finding suitable aged care support. Users can search geographical areas to find local aged care services and can access an interactive 'vacancy register' which shows current residential aged care vacancies.

DPS Guide to Aged Care and Website

Published yearly with issues for each state and territory, the *DPS Guide to Aged Care* is a directory of information on residential aged care, community living and health.

The associated website—AgedCareGuide.com.au —provides details of home and aged care facilities including an extensive list of bed vacancies in high or low-level aged care, as well as access to an online shop for aged care products.

Find My Retirement Home

www.findmyretirementhome.com.au is an independent advisor and buyer's agent specialising in retirement village homes. They can help retirees to make an informed decision on their retirement home purchase.

Millennium Aged Care Placement Consultants

Millennium is an independent organisation specialising in providing placement solutions for people moving into aged care. The service is designed to ease the transition into aged care for the potential residents and their families by providing advice, support and advocacy.

Retirement Living Online

www.retirementlivingonline.com.au is another web-based resource, providing information on retirement villages, serviced apartments, independent living alternatives and supported accommodation throughout Australia.

Directory Guide

RESIDENTIAL AGED CARE SEARCH

Step 1: Go to www.agedcareonline.com.au

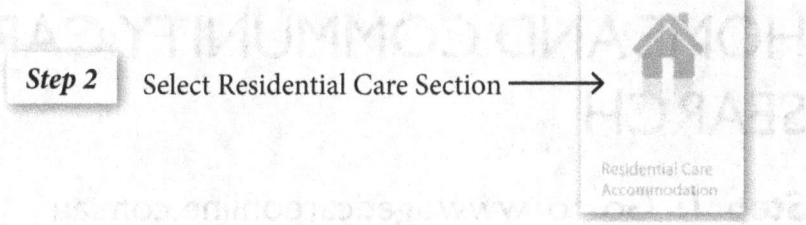

Step 2 — Select Residential Care Section ⟶

Step 3: Select the Geographical Region and Care Type (Low Care, High Care or SRS)

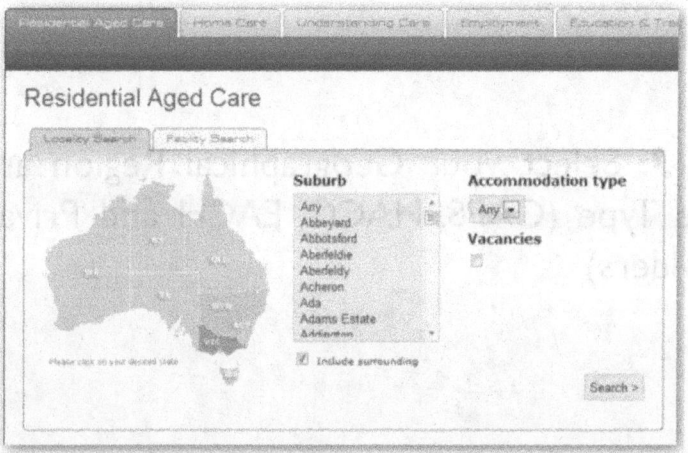

Step 4: Review the aged care providers, matching your search criteria. *Includes: Bed Numbers,*

Vacancy Information, Facility Profiles with images, Virtual Tours and Contact Details.

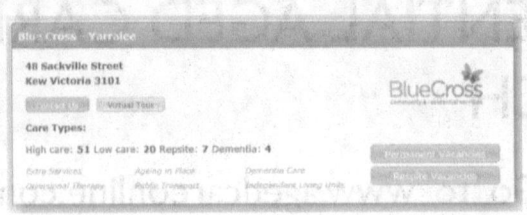

HOME AND COMMUNITY CARE SEARCH

Step 1: Go to www.agedcareonline.com.au

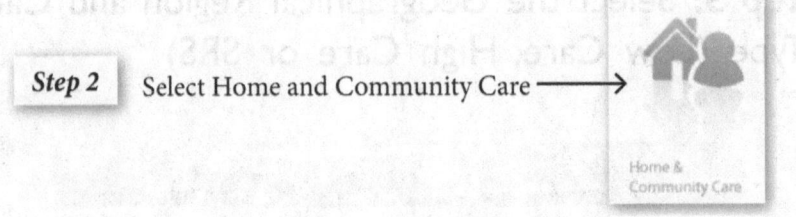

Step 3: Select your Geographical Region and Care Type (CAPS, HACC, EACH and Private Providers)

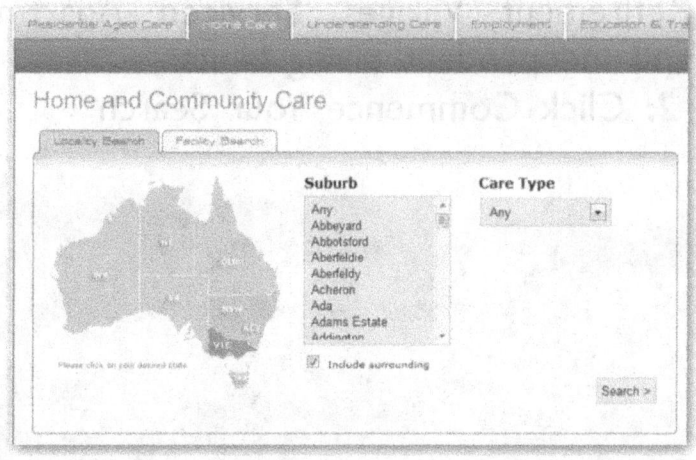

Step 4: Review the aged care providers, matching your search criteria. Includes: *Home Care provider details with images and text, Home Care Services Regions and Contact Details.*

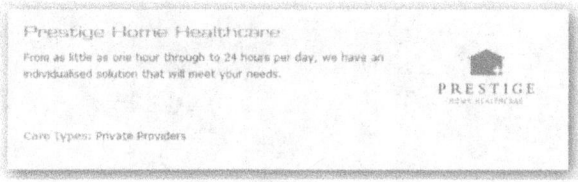

RETIREMENT VILLAGES SEARCH

Step 1: Go to www.retirementlivingonline.com.au

Retirement Living Online provides a comprehensive directory of retirement living accommodation across Australia including

Retirement Villages, Serviced Apartments and Independent Living Units.
***Step* 2:** Click Commence Your Search

***Step* 3:** Select the Region

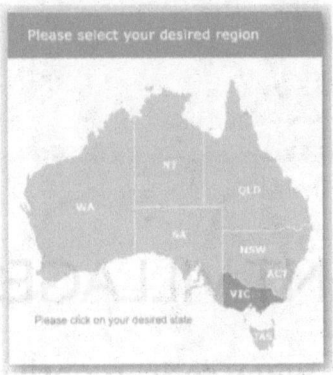

***Step* 4:** Review the retirement living providers, matching your search criteria. Includes:
Retirement Living Profiles with descriptions and text, Properties for sale, Virtual Tours and Contact Details.

Glossary

Aged Care Assessment Team (ACAT)—health professionals such as doctors, nurses, and others. You require ACAT Assessment to access government funded aged care services. The assessment determines the level and types of services for which you are eligible. The outcome is provided in writing and is referred to as the Aged Care Client Record (ACCR).

Aged Care Funding Instrument (ACFI)—replaced the Resident Classification System (RCS) on 20 March 2008. The ACFI defines a resident's care needs as nil, low, medium or high in the areas of activities of daily living, behaviours and complex healthcare. The ACFI is the instrument through which aged care facilities receive funding from the government.

Aged Care Complaints Investigation Scheme (CIS)—takes information and complaints about the delivery of government funded aged care in the home or in an aged care facility. CIS has the power to investigate the complaint and require the service provider to take action to fix the issue.

Aged Care commissioner—is responsible for independently reviewing the way in which CIS handles complaints and reviewing CIS decisions, processes and procedures.

Aged Care Standards and Accreditation Agency—is responsible for approving and monitoring compliance of aged care facilities with the accreditation standards set out in the *Aged Care Act 1997*.

Accommodation bond—the amount payable for permanent entry to a low care or extra service facility. The accommodation bond can be paid by lump sum, periodical payment or a combination of the two. The amount of accommodation bond paid to an approved provider (less any retention) is guaranteed by the government.

Accommodation charge—the daily fee payable for permanent entry to a high care facility for residents who are not fully supported. The amount of accommodation charge payable will depend on your level of assessable assets and is fixed at the date of permanent entry.

Accreditation—aged care facilities are required to comply with the accreditation standards set out in the *Aged Care Act 1997* to be eligible to receive government funding.

Ageing in Place—aged care facilities which are able to offer increased care as a resident's care needs change, enabling them to stay in the same facility, e.g. moving from low care to high care.

Asset assessment (Request for Assets Assessment booklet)—also referred to as "The Blue Book", a declaration of assets provided to Centrelink/Department of Veterans' Affairs to determine the assessable assets and the maximum amount of accommodation bond or accommodation charge a resident can be asked to pay.

Assessable assets—your assessable assets for aged care purposes include all of your assets both within Australia and overseas but not your home in all cases. See Chapter 13 for details.

Asset cut-off level—there are two asset cut-off levels for supported residents. For fully supported residents the asset cut-off level is equal to the minimum assets amount (2.25 times the basic pension). As at 1 January 2011 this amount is $38,500. For partially supported residents the asset cut-off level as at 1 January

2011 is $98,237.60. Residents with assessable assets above this threshold will not be considered to be supported residents.

Booked respite—the facility can offer respite stays for those with an eligible ACAT assessment.

Commonwealth Respite and Carelink Centre—provides information about aged and disability care services available within Australia. They can put you in contact with the ACAT team in your area.

Community Aged Care Package (CACP)—provides ACAT assessed low level care services in a home setting. Services can include personal care, domestic assistance and transport.

Consumer Directed Care packages (CDC)—provide community care services in a home setting with a greater level of control and flexibility of the services received by the recipient.

Couples accommodation—the facility has rooms large enough to accommodate a couple or has interconnecting rooms.

Cultural/ethnic specific—the facility caters to residents of one or more ethnic groups. Particular dietary requirements and ethnic traditions may be observed.

Daily care fee—also known as the basic daily care fee, this is payable by residents of residential aged care facilities in low care, high care and extra services. Daily care fees vary depending on whether you are: standard residents, protected residents, phased residents and/or non-standard residents.

Day Therapy Centre (DTC)—provides a range of rehabilitation and care services to enable people to continue living in their own home or low care facility. Services can include physiotherapy, speech therapy, occupational therapy and podiatry. Some transitional care services may also be provided.

Deeming/deemed income—the calculation of income from financial investments: bank accounts, shares, managed funds etc. by Centrelink/DVA which is not based on actual income but according to deeming rates.

Deferred Management Fee (DMF)—also referred to as a "departure fee" or "exit fee", is the fee payable when you leave a Retirement Village (and in some cases demountable homes park). The amount is often based on a formula that determines a percentage of either the purchase price or sale price based on how long you have lived in the village. The formula may provide for a split of any capital gain. In addition to the formula there may be fixed costs for refurbishments.

Dementia Specific—the facility caters to residents with dementia or similar conditions, either across the whole service or in a designated area.

Department of Health and Ageing (DoHA)—the Department of Health and Ageing has a diverse range of responsibilities including overseeing the funding and accreditation of aged care services.

Director of Nursing (DoN)—the Director of Nursing is responsible for the supervision of care across all residents of an aged care facility. He/She will liaise with doctors, nurses and other health professionals for the delivery of care services and ensure that accreditation, health and safety requirements are being met.

Diversional therapy—the facility provides diversional therapy services to residents. These services may be provided by the staff or can include external service providers.

Entry contribution—the amount payable on permanent entry to a retirement village or in establishing a granny flat right.

Extended Aged Care at Home (EACH)—provides ACAT assessed high-level care services in a home setting. Services can include personal care, domestic assistance and registered nursing care.

Extended Aged Care at Home Dementia (EACHD)—provides ACAT assessed high level care services in a home setting to people with behavioural and psychological problems associated with dementia.

Extra services—the provision of extra services is approved by the government on the basis that a higher level of accommodation and/or hotel type services is being provided. Extra Service accommodation generally is a single room with ensuite but in some cases can include private balconies/courtyards. The services can include wine with meals, daily newspaper, hairdressing, massage, podiatry etc. Residents will generally be asked to pay an extra services fee in addition to their daily care fee.

Facility pets—the facility has a resident pet(s): dog, cat, bird etc. for the enjoyment of residents.

Facility transport—the facility has its own transport (normally a bus and driver) for the benefit of residents.

Financial hardship assistance—residents of an aged care facility who have genuine difficulty meeting their cost of care can apply to the Department of Health and Ageing for financial hardship assistance. Financial hardship assistance can relate to the daily care fee and income tested fees or the accommodation bond or accommodation charge.

Home and Community Care Packages (HACC)—provide care services in a home setting. Services can include personal care, domestic assistance, meals on wheels, transport and social support. An ACAT Assessment is not required to access these services.

High care facility—formerly known as "nursing homes", provide accommodation and services to people who have been assessed as requiring high level care.

Income tested fee—the daily fee payable by residents whose income exceeds the income tested fee threshold. Income tested fees are calculated at 41.67c per dollar of income in excess of the threshold and capped at the lesser of the cost of care or $64.69 per day.

Low care—(formerly known as hostels) provide accommodation and services to people who have been assessed as having low care needs. Many low care facilities have ageing in place to cater for residents as their care needs increase.

Minimum assets amount—the amount of assets a resident must be left with when calculating the amount of accommodation bond or accommodation charge payable.

Maximum Permissible Interest Rate (MPIR)—the maximum interest rate that can be charged on any amount of unpaid accommodation bond or accruing accommodation charge liabilities. The rate is set as at the date of permanent entry, with different rates for accommodation bond and accommodation charge agreements. For accommodation bond agreements the amount of interest payable each month (together with any retention amount if appropriate) is known as the periodic payment.

Multi-Purpose Service (MPS)—provides a range of services in rural and regional areas where individual services would be unviable. These can include hospital care, mental health care, respite care and aged care. Services might also include physiotherapy, podiatry, occupational therapy as well as services provided in the community or home such as HACC packages, meals on wheels etc.

Non-standard resident—a resident who was living in aged care prior to 20 March 2008 and who was not a pensioner and paid a bond in excess of the government threshold at the time or did not disclose their financial information.

Placement consultant/agent—assists in finding an aged care facility (and in some cases can also assist with other retirement living options) for you/your loved one.

Periodical payment—the monthly payment of interest on any amount of unpaid accommodation bond (together with any retention amount if appropriate).

Phased resident—a resident who entered an aged care facility on a permanent basis on or after 20 September 2009 and is a part pensioner or self-funded retiree with private income in excess of the threshold.

Protected resident—a resident who was a permanent resident of an aged care facility on or before 19 September 2009 and is a part pensioner or self-funded retiree with private income in excess of the threshold.

Resident Classification Scale (RCS)—prior to 20 March 2008 the allocation of funding to aged care providers was based on the Resident Classification Scale. The scale ranked a resident's care needs between 1 and 8, with 1 being the highest care needs.

Resident pets—the village or facility may allow residents to bring their own pets with agreement from the management. This will depend on the type of pet, nature, size and care needs.

Residential Care Agreement (RCA)—a legal agreement/contract between you and the aged care facility that documents the type of care to be provided (low care, high care, extra services), the amount of accommodation bond (if applicable) and method of payment, the ongoing fees and charges as well as your rights and responsibilities (including circumstances in which you can be asked to leave the facility) and the rights and responsibilities of the facility management.

Respite care—these services can be in-home services for a few hours or overnight, day care services in the community or short stays in a residential aged care facility.

Retention—the monthly amount that may be deducted from the accommodation bond (currently $307.50p.m.) for the length of stay up to a maximum of five years. Where an accommodation bond is unpaid, the retention amount may be added to the interest and charged monthly; this is known as a Periodical Payment.

Retirement village—a purpose built community for people over a certain age (generally 55) which operates under the *Retirement Villages Act* in that state or territory.

Secure garden—the facility has secure garden areas for people with dementia or similar behaviours.

Serviced apartment—provides services such as meals, laundry and domestic assistance and may include some care services to an apartment within a retirement village setting.

Spouse without an ACAT—also referred to as "unfunded residents". The facility will enable a couple to move into the aged care facility with one member of the couple not having an ACAT. As the facility will not receive any ACFI for the person without the ACAT, a payment arrangement outside the normal fees and charges will probably apply.

Standard resident—a resident who has private income below the threshold. They may have been in care prior to 20 September 2009 or moved into care after this date.

Supported living—a retirement village, caravan park or demountable homes park that provides residents with access to support services such as meals, laundry and domestic assistance and may include some care services.

Supported resident—there are two types of supported residents: fully supported and partially supported. Fully supported residents are those with assessable assets below the minimum assets amount (currently $39,000) and who do not pay an accommodation bond or charge. Partially supported residents are those with assets above the minimum assets amount but below the upper asset cut off level (currently $102,544) and who pay a calculated amount of accommodation bond or charge. Aged care facilities (with the exception of extra services) are required to maintain a ratio of supported residents to be eligible to receive funding from the government.

Supported Residential Service (SRS)—provides care services that may be similar to that of a residential aged care facility to the aged and disabled with funding provided by the state government.

24-hour monitored supervision—the resident has an electronic call bell or intercom system that enables them to request assistance from a member of staff 24 hours per day.

24-hour on-site supervision—qualified personal care staff or nurses supervising residents 24 hours per day.

Transitional Care—short-term care provided after a hospital stay to assist the person to continue living in their own home. Transitional care can be provided in a hospital, aged care facility, community centre or your own home.

Veterans' Home Care package—provides care services to eligible veterans and war widow/ers in a home setting. Services can include personal care, domestic assistance, home and garden maintenance and respite care. A Veterans' Home Care assessment is required to access these services.

Do you need even more information?

> Then visit our website

www.agedcarewhocares.com.au

Contact an aged care specialist through the site, as well as access other resources:

- placement consultants
- retirement village and aged care directories
- links to up-to-date aged care fees and charges and
- a calendar of events.

Back Cover Material

"Older Australians have real choices today in how they live their lives as they progress into their senior years and how they wish to utilize the care and support available to them. However the range of options and choices can be confusing and this book performs an excellent role in steering the reader through. The authors have distilled a highly complex and often bewildering topic into an informative and enjoyable read. It is a great resource for the elderly and their families, as well as all staff working in the aged care industry."

Rod Young
CEO, Aged Care Association Australia

RACHEL LANE is the Executive Manager—Aged Care Solutions for Colonial First State. Having worked in financial services for 12 years and as a specialist in aged care for the past seven years, she is well known and respected within these industries, particularly for providing advice on the structuring of assets and income for aged care residents.

NOEL WHITTAKER is one of Australia's best known financial advisers and is a founding director of Whittaker Macnaught Pty Ltd, a leading financial planning organisation. He is a pioneer in the field of consumer education and is the author of 19 books including the international best seller *Making Money Made Simple*. He writes weekly columns in many major Australian newspapers, and also makes regular appearances on radio and television.

Index

A
ACAT assessment, *23, 24*
Accommodation bonds, *138, 140, 141, 143, 144, 145, 147, 150, 153, 214, 216, 217, 219, 221, 223*
Accommodation charge, *140*
Accreditation, *85*
Aged care classifications, *82, 83*
Aged Care Complaints Investigation Scheme (CIS), *136*
Ageing in Place (AIP), *80*
Annuities, *207, 209, 210, 212*
Assessable assets formula, *117*
Asset test exempt income streams, *165*
Assets assessment process, *111*

C
Care in own home, *15, 16, 19, 21*
Certification, *85*
CIS, *136*
Commonwealth Rent Assistance, *47, 49*
Community nursing programs, *19, 21*
Company structure or trust, *196, 197, 199, 200, 201, 203, 205*
Company title, *52*
Complaints, *136*
Complying income streams, *114*
Conversion factor-granny flat, *9, 12*
Costs of moving, *132, 135*
Criteria and standards, *83*

D
Daily care fee, *155, 156, 158, 160*

Deeming., *162, 164*
Deferred Management Fee, *64*
Defined benefit superannuation, *164*
Dementia specific, *92*
Demountable Homes Parks, *44, 47*

F
Farms., *114*
Financial hardship., *127*
Financial strategies, *172*
Financial supplements, *123*
Fixed term annuities, *207, 209, 210, 212*
Former home-keeping, *174, 176, 177, 178, 179*
Freehold title., *52*
Funeral bonds, *238*
Funeral costs, *236, 238, 239*

G
Gifts, *113*
Granny flat, *3, 5, 6, 8, 9, 12, 13*
Group title, *57, 60*

H
Hardship, *127*
Holiday homes, *181, 182, 183*
Home-keeping, *174, 176, 177, 178, 179*

I
Income-tested fee, *160, 161, 162*
Independent living, *33, 34*
Informal care, *13*
Investment properties, *168, 170*

K
Keeping former home, *174, 176, 177, 178, 179*

L
Leasehold title, *52*
Level of care, *100*
Licence, *52*
Lifetime annuities, *207, 209, 210, 212*
Long term income streams, *165*

M

Mortgages-reverse, *186, 187, 188, 190, 191, 193, 194*
Multi-purpose services, *92, 93*

N

Non-standard resident, *158*
Notice to leave, *50*
Notice to vacate, *50*

P

Periodic interest payment, *147*
Phased resident, *158*
Placement brokers, *105*
Police checks, *88*
Prepaying funeral, *236, 238, 239*
Private carers, *21*
Protected resident, *158*
Protection of accommodation bond, *153*
Prudential requirements-bonds, *153*

R

Reasonableness test-granny flat, *6*
Refunding bond, *150*
Rental villages, *40, 41*
Residential aged care, *78*
Residential care agreement., *129, 131*
Respite, *95*
Retention amount-bond, *145, 147*
Retirement village costs., *62, 64, 65, 67, 69, 70, 72*
Retirement villages, *26, 27, 29, 30, 33*
Reverse mortgages, *186, 187, 188, 190, 191, 193, 194*

S

Serviced apartments, *34, 36*
Short term income streams, *168*
Special services, *90, 92, 93, 95, 97, 98*
Standard resident, *158*
Strata title, *57, 60*
Strategies, *172*
Superannuation, *113*

Supported living units, *34, 36*
Supported Residential Services, *95*
Supported residents., *125, 127*

T
Taking leave, *131, 132*
Transitional care., *93*
Trust or company structure, *196, 197, 199, 200, 201, 203, 205*

U
Using a placement broker, *105*

V
Veterans' Home Care, *19, 21*
Village Life Limited, *40*

W
Waiting list and interim care, *103*
War Widows Pension, *170*

www.ingramcontent.com/pod-product-compliance
Lightning Source LLC
Chambersburg PA
CBHW011750220426
43670CB00019B/2929